I CHOOSE TO
CHANGE

Other Highland Books

by Benson Idahosa

Power for your Zero Hour

Faith can change your Destiny

edited by Christopher Catherwood

Martyn Lloyd-Jones: Chosen by God

edited by Edward England

My Call to Preach

David Watson: A Portrait by his Friends

edited by Ann England

We Believe in Healing

by Michael Green

Evangelism in the Early Church

by Michael Harper

Walk in the Spirit

by Thomas à Kempis

The Imitation of Christ

by Gordon MacDonald

Ordering your Private World

Restoring your Spiritual Passion

by John Sherrill

They Speak with other Tongues

by Jack R. Taylor

The Hallelujah Factor

by Kenneth N. Taylor

How to Grow—First steps for New Christians

by Phyllis Thompson

Gladys Aylward: A London Sparrow

by Sabina Wurmbrand

The Pastor's Wife

by Zig Ziglar

Raising Positive Kids in a Negative World

I CHOOSE TO CHANGE

THE SCRIPTURAL WAY TO SUCCESS AND PROSPERITY

by

BENSON IDAHOSA

HIGHLAND BOOKS

First Published 1987

Printed in Great Britain for
HIGHLAND BOOKS
6 The White House, Beacon Road,
Crowborough, East Sussex TN6 1AB,
by Richard Clay Ltd, Bungay, Suffolk
Typeset by CST, Eastbourne, East Sussex

CONTENTS

FOREWORD

No subject can be sure to cause so much contention among Christians today as that of prosperity. The plain truth is that God intends His children to prosper. That is the clear teaching of the Old Testament and is part of the good news revealed through Jesus Christ. He came to establish God's heavenly Kingdom on earth—and surely nobody can believe that heaven will be a place of poverty?

Benson Idahosa does not preach a 'prosperity gospel'. This is no 'get rich quick' formula. He expounds the biblical truth that prosperity is an aspect of God's purpose for His children and is to be seen alongside other aspects of His plan. God causes His children to prosper when they live by the principles of the Kingdom, exercising their faith in God's goodness.

These pages are both encouraging and challenging and are a prophetic word to Christians today, especially those with a diminished sense of God's generosity and goodness. Faith is enlarged as the revelation of God's grace unfolds.

Not only has Dr Idahosa lived by these principles for many years; his work in Nigeria is a living testimony that they work. Those who live by these Kingdom principles not only prosper themselves but overflow in generosity to others, for giving is the secret of receiving. And giving leads to many thanksgivings to God.

Praise to Him for His generous love!

Colin Urquhart

1

GOD'S WEALTH IS YOURS

You will be made rich in every way so that you can be generous on every occasion.
2 Corinthians 9.11

Many years ago, God changed my attitude to success and prosperity. I thank Him that He did. But many still languish in ignorance, unbelief and confusion on the subject. Prosperity among Christians is a topic that generates considerable argument in many quarters. All over the world, the controversy is still raging.

God created men and women for a better life than many are experiencing. It is not His will, as erroneously propagated, that we live a life of sin, guilt, near-nakedness and failure. Salvation, we must understand, satisfies all of man's fundamental needs. Hallelujah! Salvation affects the whole person, spiritually, physically and materially. All of the world's wealth is *created* by our Father. Gold, silver, diamonds, oil, cattle, all are His. The simple truth is that He created and owns it all (see Exodus 19.5).

Every born again Christian, man or woman, must fully comprehend two salient facts regarding success and failure. First, God created all the wealth on this earth and it is His. And He can by His provident will place it in your empty hands for His work's sake as you claim His promises and act upon them by faith. Secondly, God asks that we share our financial and material prosperity for His glory and for His work. Are you beginning to understand? God's plan is for you to be saved, happy, blessed, successful and prosperous! Why would God create material blessings if they were sinful? Ponder over that question. Listen, my friend, God's resources are not diminishing: they are there to be tapped. Who will tap them? You!

Victory in Christ

We are saved? From what to what? Death to life! Sin to righteousness! Darkness to light! Poverty to prosperity! Fear to faith! Failure to success! And more and more! In his book *The Good Life,* Dr T. L. Osborn states: 'God created an abundance of everything. He placed us here amidst it all. He is rich. He adopts us when we receive Christ. He wills that we enjoy His *plenty*—spiritually, physically and materially.'

There are innumerable Scriptures that tell us that God wants His children to prosper and to be blessed materially so long as our motive is right. Why? So that He can meet all of your needs and give you enough prosperity to have '*plenty left over*' to share in carrying out His will on earth. God is able to give you 'everything you need and more, so that there will not only be enough for your own needs, but plenty left over to give joyfully to others. For God, who gives seed to the farmer to plant, and later on, good crops to harvest and eat, will give you more and more seed to plant and will make it grow so that you can give away more and more fruit from your harvest. Yes, God will give you *much* so that you can give away much, and when we take your gifts to those who need them they will break out into thanksgiving and praise to God for your help' (2 Cor 9.8, 10–11 LB).

For God to 'supply all your needs' He must provide money. Christians must have money to meet their own needs and then to carry out God's will on earth. They must learn the secret of God's financial blessing as well as His spiritual and physical ones. God is good, and He longs to manifest His goodness toward you. 'Yea I will rejoice over them to do them good . . . with My whole heart and with My whole soul' (Jer 32.41)—and our God has a very big heart and a very big soul. As a born again Christian what should be your approach? Success is a road you must travel because God wishes it so (3 John 2). Be encouraged to renew your mind and thinking, according to the Master's promises. Look up and reach out for excellence.

Vision for success

The vision for achievement in all human endeavour eludes many. But you are going to catch a glimpse of it. 'And ye shall know the truth, and the truth shall make you free' (Jn 8.32). What truth are we talking about? The naked truth is that the devil is also offering you something: poverty, deprivation and failure. Reject them! Life is for living in the presence of God. Remember the words in Proverbs 23.23, 'Buy the truth, and sell it not.' Do you hear that? Truth is what I am giving to you: please don't reject it!

What are some of the mischievous lies the devil puts across to confuse people about prosperity and success? First, he suggests that material poverty fosters spiritual humility. Don't allow such a thought to reign in your heart; it is sickening and defiling. The Bible says that the blessings of the Lord make men rich. You will also hear that prosperity or the good life encourages one to arrogance, pride and sinful living. It is for you to judge whether that is true or not. Was Abraham proud when God blessed him? Did King David not still follow the commandments of God, in spite of his riches? Many affluent people are putting millions of dollars into the ministry, sending missionaries and preachers to remote areas. Does this spring from pride? And don't forget, it is not only the rich who are in danger of being infected by pride.

I have a faithful partner in the ministry who stands by me day and night. He once owned a fleet of cars, but suddenly things went wrong. Before long, all the fleet had broken down. Yet God was with him. God gave him new revelation and new direction. Did he then become proud? No! Today, he is a pillar of faith, well-known in heaven and on earth for his faithfulness to God and His calling. He is a success in every way imaginable. Praise God! Beloved, your liberation has also come. Re-examine God's dream. If God places so much value upon you, surely he wants you to benefit from the abundance of His creation. Who else has it been created for? (see Psalm 24.1). Is it wrong for someone with implicit faith in God to be blessed materially? Of course not.

Meeting God

God's abundance in this world was never intended for the few to monopolise. It is created for His people to enjoy, to utilise for the glory of God and the benefit of others. There are natural laws which God has made a part of this universe. All who apply them can become achievers and possessors. Even unbelievers who inquire and discover these laws may apply them and become winners in life. On the other hand, those believers who do not discover these laws may live their lives as physical and material losers.

God's plan is for His children to run this world and to enjoy its treasures. But He has decreed laws. Anyone who will discover them will reap their rich harvest, whether that person is a believer or an unbeliever. Jesus said: He makes the sun to rise on the evil and on the good, and sends rain on the just and on the unjust!

A believer who is undisciplined and slothful in business principles will not prosper. He or she may pray for a material miracle, but will end up with nothing. On the other hand, an unbeliever who is astute, decisive and diligent in business principles may act according to God's laws and become very successful. A believer who will not till the soil and plant the field may *seem* 'spiritual' and may pray for a miraculous harvest, but he or she will end up in poverty. An unbeliever who tills the soil and plants the field will reap a rich harvest. God is trusting us to discover His laws of success, to discipline ourselves as His family members and eventually to become the material empire-builders of His world.

God's wealth is for everyone

God never intended that anyone should go through life imprisoned by their own superstitions. He opens the door of success to every believer who will dare to step out and go after the good life. No one in God's family was ever destined to exist in sickness, fear, ignorance, poverty, loneliness or mediocrity. God's abundant goodness will be enjoyed and utilised by those who discipline themselves, become decisive, bold, adventurous, believing, daring, risking and determined. It belongs to those who dare to set high goals, determine to persevere and handle responsibly the share of the material world that God has entrusted to them.

Once you have set your eyes on God's lifestyle, you will no longer cower and retreat when the going gets rough. You will transform each problem into an opportunity for growth. You will dream greater dreams than ever and, with God's help, you will make those dreams come true. If your hopes are dashed by opposition you will not cringe in fear of judgment. Instead you will pick up the pieces, learn by your mistakes, profit by learning your enemy's strategy and set even higher targets the next time around.

The Bible will vibrate with new meaning: They that seek the Lord shall not want any good thing (Ps 34.10). The Lord is your shepherd, you shall not want (Ps 23.1). The Lord your God brings you into a good land of brooks and fountains and springs, of wheat and barley and vines and fig trees and pomegranates, of olive oil and honey; a land where you shall eat bread without scarceness and you shall not lack anything (Deut 8.7–9).

2

DREAMING GOD'S DREAMS

Seek first his kingdom and his righteousness and all these things will be given to you as well.
Matthew 6.33

Dreaming impossible dreams is a habit of mine: aspiring to the good things God has created in this world is my ambition. I don't regret it: God placed me here to work in partnership with Him. I dream big; I aspire to achieve by His grace and I drive towards my goal. This is why many projects in my ministry, originally dismissed as impossible, have come to fruition after all. When you glimpse God's abundance, created for you, you will never be the same again.

Many believers take time to think about heaven. Heaven is a place of plenty. And Jesus said, 'Thy will be done on earth as it is in heaven.' That is God's will! His wealth on earth was created to work for the good. God does not need to hold on to the treasures He placed on the earth, because He has still an abundance in heaven! The Bible declares that God rewards faith *now*, as well as in heaven. Let your mind be renewed and miracles will begin to take place in your life. Success is coming your way in Christ, who became poor that you might be rich.

Until we have a dream, we can never know what it is to have a dream come true. The pious religious person turns his back on our needs, saying that they arise from wrong desires. To do this is like lopping off our feet because we want shoes! But the Bible says that, by God's mighty power at work within us, He is able to do far more than we would dare to ask or even dream of—infinitely beyond our highest prayers, thoughts or hopes (Eph 3.20 LB). Aspire to all that God has created; let go of all religious taboos regarding material blessings and happiness. You deserve the best in life. That is why God created it and put you here in the middle of it. It is your domain.

People who accuse the prosperous and condemn the affluent often hoard and conceal their miserly stocks for their own futures, never enjoying the pleasure of God's material blessing in the now, and certainly never helping others. This world and its wealth is our domain. But we can never possess this pearl of great price until first we understand its value and then aspire to possess it, for the blessing of other people around us and for the glory of God.

We are stewards

God entrusts every generation with seeds to plant, soil to cultivate, oceans to sail, mountains to scale, deserts to conquer, rivers to harness, minerals to mine and forests to utilise. He also gives each of us a brain and a spirit with which to receive His creative ideas. With Him at work in us we can *be, have* and *do,* anything He puts into our spirit and mind. We are to be the masters of this world. Jesus told us to ask, seek, knock. Everyone that asks receives (Mt 7.7–8). How simple! If you want something enough to ask, to seek and to knock, you will get it.

Jesus said to a woman who intensely wanted Him to heal her daughter and who would not give up: 'Be it as you desire' (Mt 15.28). And the girl was healed. When you delight in God, He gives you the desires of your heart. You will inherit the earth. God will exalt you to inherit the land (Ps 37.4, 9, 34). There is plenty of everything for you, if you are convinced of your own value in God's eyes and really aspire to the best in life.

Full of hope

Something inside you is saying, 'From today, no person, demon or system is going to restrict and restrain me, condemn and confuse me, judge and abuse me, or manipulate and manoeuvre me.' From now on, you will have a more positive and hopeful attitude to life:

> *I can expect God's best because He created it for me.*
> *I can expect good news because He sends it to me.*
> *I can expect happiness because He fashioned me.*
> *I can expect exhilarating health because His goodness is all around me.*
> *I can expect genuine love because He forgave me.*
> *I can expect a positive uplift because He inspires me.*

You are already beginning to touch and experience the exhilarating life that God created for you.

You are made for life and not for death.
You are made for health and not for disease.
You are made for success and not for failure.
You are made for faith and not for confusion.
You are made for love and not for fear.

You are discovering that God wants your life to represent all of the good that He is and that He has created. After all, you have done what Jesus said you should do: you have sought first the Kingdom of God. You have discovered that God's plan is to set up His love headquarters in your house. You have sought your right standing in this Kingdom. You have discovered that you and God are co-workers in His powerful plan of love. You have accepted His promise that all these good things shall be added to you (Mt 6.33). You have learned to see yourself as God sees you. You have discovered that you are God's life at work in the present. You have discovered the wonder of His grace. You have learned to affirm:

I am part of God's plan.
I am vital to His dream.
I am an instrument in His kingdom.
I am a member of His family.
I am the proof of God's love.
I am the evidence of His life.
I am the form of His body.
I am the temple of His Spirit.
I am the expression of God's faith.

I am the fruit of His life.
I am the action of His plan.
I am the example of His seed.

Your entire outlook on life is different. You declare:

God made me.
God believes in me.
God loves me.
God paid for me.
God never gives up on me.
God gave His Son for me.
God redeemed me.
God values me.

You are breathing fresh air. You are hearing new music. A new song is born in you.

All things are possible to believers in Christ (1 Jn 5.12–14). The person who believes is transformed (Mk 9.23). Decide to live up to your full potential. Your choice is very important. You cannot afford to fail. To fail, you must quit first; to quit you must decide not to continue. But the will of God is that you prosper and be in good health (3 Jn 1.2). Realise that God says you are His own branch (Jn 15.5); you can turn from being a beggar to a master (Mt 6.33)—if you seek His Kingdom. Hallelujah!

I can hear God saying to you, 'Son, daughter, I have done all I could to help you succeed. I gave Jesus, I gave you His name, I gave you His power, His love, His authority and wisdom (Jn 14.14–15). Now it's up to you! The Kingdom of God is within you. Look to God and His Kingdom, and your dreams can then become reality. Choose to change from fear to faith, from poverty to riches, from failure to success, from bondage to freedom, from sickness to health. You are downcast—God will uplift you; you are sitting still—God wants you to travel the world with the good news of Him! Our God reigns; He brings you from discouragement to new courage, from fainting to strength. Be strong, I hear God say to you, be very courageous. Be bold, be thick-skinned, be wise. Above all, be optimistic.

3

FEAR THE LORD AND BE FAITHFUL

Blessed is the man who fears the Lord, who finds great delight in his commands . . . wealth and riches are in his house, and his righteousness endures for ever.

Psalm 112.1,3

One of the greatest discoveries for new Christians is the realisation that wealth is of God and that it is His will that they should prosper for His work's sake. After you have made that initial discovery, you must act upon your faith. To put faith into action is the secret which leads to the fulfilment of all God's promises (Jas 2.14–17, 26). The sequence of events is something like this:

1. God gives the promise.
2. We hear it, believe it, and accept it as God's revealed will.
3. We ask God to fulfil His promise.
4. We act on the Word of promise, proving by our action that we believe God will do as He said.
5. God sees our action, which justifies our faith before Him, and He steps into the scene to fulfil His promise.

6. The devil (God's enemy and ours) steps in to create doubt, fear, confusion or hesitation in order to delay or prevent God's fulfilment and our joy.
7. As our faith remains unwavering under trial, God's covenant cannot fail and He makes His Word good, for 'He watches over His Words to perform them' (Jer 1.12). 'No Word from God is void of power' (Lk 1.37 RV). [His] 'covenant will [He] not break nor alter the thing that is gone out of [His] lips,' (Ps 89.34) for 'the Scripture cannot be broken,' (Jn 10.35) and 'Heaven and earth shall pass away but My Word shall never pass away' (Mk 13.31).

So, standing upon the rock of God's promises which reveal His will, you, as a partner in soul-winning, can step out by faith. You can claim His prosperity to do His will on earth, which is to give the Gospel to others. God always demands that we *act* our faith first. This proves our believing. Then He steps into the scene to make good His promise. For example, a woman in the Bible was in debt and her creditors were coming to take her sons as slaves, for payment. The prophet ordered her to act her faith. She borrowed many empty vessels, then took the only pot of oil she had and poured it out. That was her faith in action. Her oil never failed and she was miraculously put into a thriving oil business that prospered so well that every debt was paid in full and she was told: 'Live, thou and thy children, of the rest' (2 Kg 4.1–7).

God doesn't need an oil well to put you into the oil business, or a larger farm to increase your supply of meal. God is not limited to your income, or farm, or salary, or business, or stocks, or securities, or pension or interest. All wealth is His creation. Act on His Word. Claim His fulfilment. He has a million ways to place wealth into your hands. God can do financial miracles as easily as spiritual or physical ones. If God can save a sinner or heal a blind man, is He limited in giving you financial prosperity? I could recount hundreds of almost unbelievable ways God has prospered Christians who have stepped by faith into an enlarged ministry of giving. Those who do not understand this principle frown on someone of limited resources who gives money for the Lord's work. They forget Jesus' commendation of the widow who gave her last mite into the treasury (Mk 12.41–44).

Many Christians have fallen prey to the biting accusations of the world. 'Christians are not supposed to have money!' is the battle cry they hear. Because someone used a knife to kill, would you conclude that we must not use a knife to peel an orange? Or if a man drowns in the river should his family stop drinking water? These statements are no more illogical than the suggestion that because money is sometimes used wrongly Christians should shun prosperity. There are indeed many people who have acquired wealth illegally. But you cannot deny the fact that there are also many genuine and sincere rich people in this world today.

Some believe that money is the root of all evil. God's inspired Word on this is given in 1 Timothy 6.10: 'For the *love* of money is the root of all evil, which while some coveted after, they have erred from the faith, and pierced themselves through with many evils.' The Bible doesn't say that to *have* money is to have evil; but to be possessed by the *love* of money is wrong. Make an idol of money and you give first place to the devil rather than God. To turn away from God, *this* is the root of all evil. I am absolutely certain that it is the will of God for His children to prosper, because the Scripture says so and gives ample proof of this position. There are only two categories of people in the world; the achievers and failures, winners and losers. In other words, those who are succeeding and those who are failing. Those who are well and those who are sick. The righteous and the unrighteous! You know as well as I do that these two categories of people have been in existence from the time of creation and they will continue to exist.

So the first question to pose is this: is it the will of God for Christians to achieve success and acquire wealth? The problem with many people is that they judge situations by worldly standards, they prefer advocating austerity to placing their faith in God.

You are God's human representative

God's life is in you! Take a look at these Scriptures and you will see:

> *Your life is hid with Christ in God, Christ is your life* (Col 3.3–4).
> *Christ is in you* (Col 1.27).
> *Christ lives in you* (Gal 2.20).
> *It is God who works in you* (Phil 2.13).
> *You will know that you are in me and that I am in you* (Jn 14.20).
> *Hereby you know that you dwell in God and*

He in you (1 Jn 4.13).
He abides in you (1 Jn 3.14).
Now you are God's own (1 Pet 2.10).
You are an heir of God and a joint heir with Christ (Rom 8.17).
You are the temple of God (1 Cor 3.16).
With God at work you go from blessing to blessing, you bear more fruit (Jn 15.2).
By this the Father is glorified (Jn 15.8).

Possibly some will say, 'Archbishop Idahosa, you have no problem because you are known all over the world.' That may well be, but the world is not my source and anchor, Jesus Christ is! Even if I am not known all over the world, I am known in heaven. Heaven is the one place where I am definitely known and recognised, and it must also be your focal point. King David, the servant of God, said 'From whence cometh my help?' He did not say his help came from the government or from a millionaire friend somewhere, or even from the biggest bank in town. David said his help came from the Lord God, who made heaven and earth. Do you agree with that? Do you agree that the Lord God Almighty made heaven and earth (Ps 24.1)? It is a foundational truth. The Bible declares that the two richest men in Old Testament times were Abraham and Solomon. King David was succeeded by King Solomon who must have been one of the richest men in history (1 Kg 10).

I read in my Bible an important verse you need to look at: you will find it in Ecclesiastes 5.19: 'Every man also to whom God hath given riches and wealth, and hath given him power to eat thereof, and to take his portion, and to rejoice in his labour. This is the gift of God.' I am sure you read as I did that riches and wealth are from God. Before I deal with the next point, I wish to draw your attention to Proverbs 10.22 which reads, 'The blessing of the Lord, it maketh rich, and addeth no sorrow with it.' Money received through tax evasion, bribes and all illegal methods is not from God and therefore comes under judgment. It is from the devil!

The money that God will be served by is the money that God Himself gave you power to receive through hard work, through creativity, through labour, good works and the light of the Gospel. For many businessmen in our country, Christians and unbelievers alike, the thorniest area has to do with the award of contracts. You may read these words and say, 'Well, if God was not with me and happy with me, why did I win that big contract?' Beloved, the crucial factor is *how* you went about winning that big contract with the huge dividends. Does the scheming and bribery that won you the contract sound safe and defensible before God and His Word (Col 3.17)? You need to be reminded again that a day is coming when everyone, none excepted, will give an account before God Almighty.

I often sit back and thank God that believing Christians can have riches and wealth, which the Bible states are gifts of God. God wants riches to come from Him as your sole source and provider. Study and meditate on Psalm 112.1–3, 'Praise ye the Lord. Blessed is the man that feareth the Lord . . . . wealth and riches shall be in his house; and his righteousness endureth forever.' Praise the Lord!

4

CHOOSING TO FOLLOW GOD

For the Lord God is a sun and shield; the Lord bestows favour and honour; no good thing does he withhold from those whose walk is blameless.

Psalm 84.11

What is the first secret to learn, therefore, if you long to attain the riches and wealth of the Lord? First, the fear of the Lord. Secondly, learn to delight in Him. Thirdly, obey His commandments. 'They that fear the Lord and serve the living God,' says the Bible, 'shall never lack any good thing.' Fear the Lord, delight in Him by daily obedience to His commandments: then you can be sure that wealth and riches will be yours. I thank God for what Jesus said in Matthew 6.33, 'Seek ye first the Kingdom of God and His righteousness, and all these things shall be added unto you.' To seek the Kingdom of God is to renounce the works of the enemy.

Many today are seeking the wealth of the devil, others are seeking the kingdom of the devil (Satan) with which he tempted Jesus in the wilderness (Lk 4; Mt 4). But praise the Lord, we will serve the living Lord our God, who has power to give us riches and wealth. 1 Chronicles 29.12 reads, 'Both riches and honour come of thee and thou reignest over all; and in thine hand is power and might.' There is an even more striking verse in Psalm 35.27, 'Let them shout for joy, and be glad . . . Let the Lord be magnified, which *hath pleasure in the prosperity of His servant.*' Show that one to those who stand against Christian prosperity!

If Christians intend to help accomplish God's most important task on earth—that of taking the Gospel to every nation—they are going to have to get rid of the religious tradition that money is evil and poverty is sacred. Money in itself is not evil; 'The *love* of money is the root of all evil' (1 Tim 6.10) and 'Riches and wealth are the gift of God' (Ecc 5.19). Jesus told us to 'Seek first the expansion of God's Kingdom world-wide, and all these things shall be added unto you' (Mt 6.33 RV). You see, God promised to meet all your needs when you serve His purpose and carry out His will; 'My God shall supply all your needs according to His riches in glory by Christ Jesus' (Phil 4.19); 'No good thing will He withhold from them that walk uprightly before Him' (Ps 84.11). Jesus promised: 'What things soever ye desire, when ye pray believe that ye receive them and ye shall have them' (Mk 11.24).

For your needs to be met, you must have money. For God to supply all of your needs, He must cause you to acquire money. He did exactly that in the Bible and He will do so today. The Bible teaches that God has not changed (Mal 3.6); He is the great 'I AM' (Ex 3.14–15). 'Jesus Christ is the same yesterday, today and forever' (Heb 13.8). If you could read the prayer requests that come to us in the mail, you would understand that people have many material needs. They write to us and ask us to pray with them and for them to receive these things because they know we believe that God will do material miracles to confirm His promises of material blessings, the same as He will do spiritual or physical miracles to confirm promises of spiritual or physical blessings. We pray with faith for these blessings and God answers prayer (Jn 14.13–14).

Some Christians cannot go to their pastors for prayer about material things because religious tradition holds that 'temporal' and 'material' needs are worldly and that if they were met, one might become proud and abandon one's faith in God. People from all over the world write to us and request prayer that God will provide money to pay their bills, to get a car, to buy a house, or rent an apartment. They want a job, or better clothes, or a better business. They need money for a trip, business venture, industrial or business tools; for repairs on their house or car or equipment. They request prayer that God will intervene in their financial need for medicine, hospital care, dental work, glasses; for cattle, sheep, poultry or other farm animals; for crop planting, cultivating, disinfecting or harvesting; for repairs or new ventures; for funds to move from one place to another; for a train trip or for gasoline—for a thousand and one material needs.

They ask us to pray about these needs and our daily post also bears abundant evidence that God answers those prayers and meets those material needs—often by unexplainable miracles (Jer 32.17, 27). Aside from the spiritual needs of people, most of their needs require money. 'Things' cost money.

God created all of the wealth of this earth—not for unbelievers to monopolise, but for the prosperity of His children who do His will. So God is interested in your temporal and material needs too. The Bible contains innumerable promises for financial and material prosperity. But theologians have rarely mentioned them to us. They have majored on the negative side of the subject: that 'the love of money is the root of all evil' (1 Tim 6.10); that 'he that loveth silver shall not be satisfied with silver' (Ecc 5.10); that it is 'hard for them that trust in riches to enter the Kingdom of God' (Mk 10.24).

The rich man rejected Jesus and 'was very sorrowful; for he was very rich' (Lk 18.23). 'He that trusteth in his riches shall fail' (Prov 11.28). 'They that will be rich will fall into temptation and a snare, and into many foolish and hurtful lusts, which drown men in destruction and perdition' (1 Tim 6.9). 'Riches are deceitful' (Mt 13.22). These and many other scriptures constitute the negative side of the subject—and their admonitions should be carefully heeded. But to get God's perspective of money, we must understand that money *in itself* is not evil. It is 'the *love* of money' that is 'the root of all evil.' While God never intended that His people live in poverty, neither did He ever intend that they 'set their heart on the things of this world' (Col 3.1–2).

We are consistently warned not to '*trust* in uncertain riches' (1 Tim 6.17), and 'if riches increase, set not thine heart upon them' (Ps 62.10). This is why Jesus emphasised 'how hard it is for them that trust in riches to enter the Kingdom of God (Mk 10.24–25). We are to 'trust in God' (Ps 37.3). When someone trusts in wealth (Ps 20.7), he fails to see his need to trust in God. His whole perspective becomes distorted by the false security of his 'uncertain' riches which can be so easily wiped out. Yet it is sad that we automatically assume wealthy people to be wicked, carnal or backslidden. You cannot be wealthy *and* be spiritual, we tend to think. Forget it—that is the devil's lie! After all, King David said, 'The Lord is pleased when we are rich' (Ps 35.27). I don't know where some Christians (and unbelievers) get the idea that Christians are to go wretched, half-naked or dressed in rags. It is contrary to what the Bible says: God delights in the prosperity of His people.

Make your decision—choose your way

Are you going to walk God's way? Read the following verses from Psalm 119:

You obey His decrees (8).
You have chosen the way of truth (30).
You must hold fast to His statutes (31).
Walk at liberty in Him and seek His precepts (45).
You promise to obey His words (57).

You cannot bargain with God, but you do have a choice to make. In Deut 30.19, God says: 'I set before you life and death, blessing and cursing, therefore choose life that both you and your seed may live.' Jos 24.15—'Choose you this day whom to serve. As for me and my house, we will serve the Lord.' Someone is bound to challenge you, 'Well, there are *special* people whom God created extraordinary.' It is far from true: the fact is that God creates ordinary people who by dint of hard work become extraordinary people.

Maybe a little of my own background will throw more light on this subject. When we started the ministry, which is now known worldwide, I did not even have a microphone. There was no loudspeaker, no television crew, no studio equipment. None of what you see when you visit the Miracle Centre was there in the beginning. But one thing I have always known is that I serve a living God. And this living God said, 'If you preach Me, I will provide what you need.' Step by step, little by little, we began looking forward into the future. Hand in hand with God, Christians can face opposition. Christians can face heavy trials of the enemy. We can be knocked down but we can never be knocked out. Hallelujah! We are tried, we are persecuted, smitten by trials, but never knocked out! God forbid!

Let us look at what the psalmist wrote in Psalm 37.23, 'The steps of a good man are ordered by the Lord: and He delighteth in his way. Though he fall he shall not be utterly cast down; for the Lord upholdeth him with His hands.' Not very many years ago, God gave me a message: 'If you are in any need, heaven will intervene.' Even today, heaven will intervene in your affairs if necessary. The God we talk about is not assembled by man's hand. God is a living God, who oversees all the affairs of the universe right down to the smallest detail (Mt 10.29–31; Ps 24.1).

Yes, I am talking about the God of Abraham, Isaac, and Jacob. The God of Shadrach, Meshach and Abednego, who reigns and rules in the affairs of men. He is 'a sun and shield . . . no good thing will he withhold from them that walk uprightly' (Ps

84.11). What do you visualise when you read the words ‘good thing’? A good car, good health, good job, good wife, good children? The Bible reveals that God will withhold none of these things from them that walk uprightly. What a revelation! Do you know salvation is the name of redemption through the grace of God and faith in Jesus Christ? God has said that and it is unchangeable.

5

THE FRUITS OF THE VINE

'I am the vine; you are the branches.
If a man remains in me and I in him,
he will bear much fruit.'

John 15.5

God's Kingdom contains everything that God is: His nature; His power; His love; His health; His virtue; His righteousness; His life. All that God is is within His Kingdom; you too have access to these things when you let God come home to live in you. Read these Scriptures and you will see what I mean: 'I am the vine, ye are the branches; He that abideth in me, and I in him, the same bringeth forth much fruit; for without me ye can do nothing' (Jn 15.5); 'Neither shall they say, Lo here! or Lo there! for behold, the kingdom of God is within you' (Lk 17.21).

Kingdom means 'realm', 'domain' or 'reign'. Wherever God reigns no other power can dominate. Jesus came preaching the reign of the Kingdom (Mk 1.14). He was called Emmanuel, which means 'God with us' (Mt 1.23). In Galatians 3.13 we read, 'Christ hath redeemed us from the curse of the law . . . for it is written, Cursed is everyone that hangeth on a tree.' Do you know what Christ went through for us? Christ bought us back from the devil. Christ paid the total price. Above all, God has given every believing Christian riches beyond measure through Christ Jesus (Phil 4.19).

God has stated that those who love Him will inherit all that they need. God wants you and your children to have enough to eat and clothes to put on. See Psalm 112.1–3: 'Blessed is the man that feareth the Lord, that delighteth in His commandments . . . wealth and riches shall be in his house.'

There are very many today who don't care about the source of their money. You will hear them say, 'Money is money, whatever.' It is not so according to the Bible. When you take a bribe, rob, or steal, you are handling contaminated money. 'Well,' you may say, 'I will build a mansion with it, perhaps buy a few cars . . .' It makes no difference what you do. God's Word states that the wealth of the unrighteous is kept in store for the godly. Eventually, the righteous will reign over your riches if you acquire them illegally. The positive side is that God *does* want you to be rich, *if* you abide by the following conditions:

1. Do the will of God

According to Joshua 1.7, '. . . observe to do according to all the law which Moses my servant commanded thee . . . that thou mayest prosper whithersoever thou goest.' Make it your aim to do the will of God. Then, wherever you turn, left, right, east or west, north or south, be firmly assured that you will prosper. So you can see that the riches of God upon you have something to do with your obedience.

2. Abide by the law

'Keep therefore the words of this covenant and do them, that ye may prosper in all that ye do' (Deut 29.19). What is this telling you? 'I am going to get rich by all means, fair or foul. By hook or by crook, rich I must be.' No! The Bible says that we should abide by the word of the Bible.

There is a programme on Nigerian television called Achievers. I have read and studied the life of each of the participants and as I listen to the interviews, one thing is clear: none of these prominent men was born with a silver spoon in his mouth. Each one of them struggled day and night as other men slept and dreamt their lives away. Among them are many unbelievers. Because they strove hard to make it, God gave them grace to pull through. How much more will the child of God prosper to whom God has made the promise, 'I shall bless the labour of your hands'. I thank God for His promises to us and as we act every day in faithful obedience, He is faithful who has promised (Is 55.11).

It is many years since the beginning of the ministry of Church of God Mission International. I had no idea how the ministry would develop, but my faith and trust was in God. Of one thing I was certain. I knew that the God who called me promised, 'If you do my will I shall honour my name in your life.' The Mission today stands as a reminder to all Christians of what God can do with a willing vessel. Bit by bit, little by little, we saw the hand of God in action. Even in the smallest detail God cared and demonstrated His presence as we went along. Looking back, it seems almost incredible that I have carried the Gospel of Jesus Christ to some 75 countries. God is still exalting His name today! God does not know the word setback! If you face problems, use them as opportunities to glorify His name.

3. Walk in God's way

Read 1 Kings 2.3: 'Walk in God's way, that thou mayest prosper in all that thou doest, and whithersoever thou turnest thyself thou shall prosper.' Praise the Lord! As you read the Scriptures above, two things stand out: obedience and blessings. Why is that so? The answer is that if you are walking in the ways of God, His presence goes with you every step of the way. God is the owner of the vehicle of your life. He directs the steering of your life as He desires (1 Pet 3.12). If God has said it, it cannot be anything but the truth. When God called me He told me, 'Son, you are going to carry the cross of Jesus Christ to every continent on earth.' My belief in this statement did not free me from problems. But I stood firm. When you say 'yes' to Christ living in you, amazing things begin to happen to you.

'I am the vine, you are the branches' (Jn 15.5). You are a branch of God's power and love; of His creativity and abundance. Everything that is in the vine is manifested through you. John 15.5b—'When you abide in me and I in you, you bring forth much fruit.' That is the way to get God's best out of life. Fruit-bearing is success in living. At the beginning of my ministry, I wore oversize shoes and a borrowed suit—but my focus was on God. I knew I was walking in His will and the storm did not scare me.

4. God will provide

You need to read and prayerfully meditate upon the words of Deuteronomy 28.11,12: 'And the Lord shall make thee plenteous in goods . . .' Read these words carefully and do not let them escape from your heart. There is no place in the Bible where you are told to sit back and watch wealth roll in on you. God gives you grace and power to acquire riches and wealth, but He also requires you to stand upon His Word. Only if you live in daily obedience will you see His blessings upon your way.

God has declared that His blessings do not bring sorrow with them and that is something to rejoice about. You have no doubt heard of the millionaires who are unable to sleep at night. The reasons are many. But my joy and yours is that God's wealth doesn't give us bad nights, it doesn't scare or keep us in a perpetual state of uncertainty for tomorrow. God's wealth will not cause you to worry when there is a change of government.

5. You will lack nothing

Psalm 34.10 reads: 'They that seek the Lord shall not want any good thing.' You know what good things are, don't you? Don't you long for all the inhabitants of this nation to seek the Lord so that they may lack nothing good? Isn't your heart's desire that they should have all that is good, know all that is good, believe in all that is good, and trust God for all that is good?

6. Daily blessings

Take a look at Psalm 68.19: 'Blessed be the Lord who daily loadeth us with benefits, even the God of our salvation.' This verse is packed with meaning for you. God says, 'You are going to be rich over and above your expectations and your blessings will overflow!' Every day God will load you with goodies. When you work for 24 years in the Civil Service and you reach retirement age, they give you retirement benefits. But when you work for God, He gives you daily benefits. The Scripture says that God will 'load' you! He broadens our vision, orders our steps and enlarges our coast. We hear him say, 'The earth is mine and the fulness thereof' (Ps 24.1).

7. God the Creator

Psalm 50.10 reads: 'For every beast of the forest is mine, and the cattle upon a thousand hills.' God is speaking here as Creator and therefore possessor of all, who can give out of His abundance to all as He wishes. The Bible says God is a God of light. Therefore, any time you attach yourself to God you are connected to light, health, purity in Christ, peace and all the spiritual benefits of heaven. Why don't you make my God your God? Repent, be regenerated and receive God's glory. Let His light shine through your whole being. As God's glory covers the earth as the waters cover the sea, so shall His power envelop you. Thousands and thousands of people have received Jesus as their Lord and personal Saviour. The power and provisions of God remain the same all over the world through the riches of His glory in Christ Jesus. Your solemn prayer should be this: 'Lord, here I am. I want you to remove all else and give me Jesus. I shall then be satisfied.'

You will already have read about Moses. Read a beautiful commentary on him in Hebrews 11.26: 'Esteeming the reproach of Christ greater riches than the treasures of Egypt; for he had respect unto the recompense of the reward.' If any man ever had the advantage of royal benefits in Pharaoh's court it was Moses. He had the finest education available; wealth, and perhaps a throne, were his for the asking. But what was Moses' ultimate choice? The Bible says, 'Choosing rather to suffer affliction with the people of God than to enjoy the pleasures of sin for a season' (Heb 11.25), Moses opted for what will last, for eternity, to be on the side of the great I AM. It is beautiful to read what happened as Moses led the children of Israel out of Egypt. The Bible says that as he departed he received the spoil of all the Egyptians. He got it all! Beloved, riches in Christ means standing where Christ is; taking sides with Him who is able to do abundantly more than you expect. Go down the streets in any major city of the world and you will be alarmed at the confusion, panic and despair on many faces. Many people are out of touch with God. They have turned down a free gift—the grace of God.

Let's look at Proverbs 8.17: 'I love them that love me and those that seek me early shall find me. Riches and honour are with me, yea durable riches and righteousness.' Seek God! The Bible says that this is the only way to wealth that will make you happy. Riches and wealth can be obtained by any means. But the peace to enjoy such wealth is determined by how they are acquired. And the riches of God are the only riches that you will never be sorry about. If you seek God early—if you say sincerely,

'Jesus come into my family, Jesus come into my home, Jesus come into my job, Jesus, I beseech you, make me your good child,' Jesus will do all this and more; for He is your shield and defender, the ever-present help in time of trouble.

Beloved, let me give you this assurance: Jesus cares much, much more than you can imagine. Now listen carefully. Your destiny will depend on just a little obedience to what you read here. We all live in trying times; many situations and ways of society have bowed under the pressure in the storm of modern life. But not God's Word! Today, many are using all kinds of methods to make money, to amass wealth. But be assured that these efforts will lead you to hell, if you don't repent and ask Jesus Christ to forgive you and come into your life. Read in 2 Chronicles 20.20, 'Believe in the Lord your God, so shall ye prosper.' It is clear that you need to trust in the Lord with all your heart and lean not unto your own understanding. Then blessings will flow into your life. Also take a look at Deuteronomy 28.1–2: 'And it shall come to pass, if thou shalt hearken diligently unto the voice of the Lord thy God to observe and to do all His commandments which I command thee this day, that the Lord thy God will set thee high above all nations of the earth. And all these blessings shall come on thee and overtake thee if thou shalt hearken unto the voice of the Lord thy God.'

Faith in action

You must be a testifier rather than a complainer. God assures you that blessings will chase after you when you go in and out obediently. You will be overtaken by blessings. That is a wonderful thought to feast your mind on. So now you know the truth! You can declare that Jesus wants you to be rich and is willing to pour out His riches as you walk in obedience to His will. Allow God alone to be your source and you will never lack. Return to God in faithfulness of heart, believing every word He says. Repent! This is a vital step to entry into His purpose, as you trust Him by faith through Jesus Christ as your personal Lord and Saviour. Praise the Lord!

6

PROSPERITY IS MORE THAN MONEY

Beloved, I wish above all things that thou mayest prosper and be in health, even as thy soul prospereth.

3 John 2

I sincerely believe you have read some foundational and fundamental truths in the first part of this book, which have strengthened your understanding about God, the Bible and prosperity, the Scriptural way.

It is not my intention to tackle prosperity within the context of money only. I want to present to you the truth that in the eyes of God and His infallible Word, prosperity transcends money. You may rightly ask, 'How do I account for that?' The Bible will speak for God!

Let me point out this clear distinction as revealed in 3 John 2: 'Beloved, I wish above all things that thou mayest prosper and be in health, even as thy soul prospereth.'

My greatest amazement comes from the awareness that certain Christians, presumably from wrong teaching, seem to think money is not good. The Scripture reference in 3 John 2 is worth your earnest attention.

Many Christians call money all sorts of names, the most prominent being 'filthy lucre.' This group of people quote verses from every book of the Bible and register their narrow viewpoint that money is evil. And so they have a weird, evil imagination wherever money is mentioned.

In all known cases the quotation at the centre of the money controversy is 1 Timothy 6.10: 'The love of money is the root of all evil.' But as we have already seen, the Apostle Paul said without mincing words that the *love of money* is the entry point of all evil. It is unpardonable for anyone to take that quotation out of context and make it say that money in itself is bad. What Paul was saying and is still true for believers is that it is a serious error to make money a god, for God warns against this in the first commandment (Ex 20.3). I can say with all confidence that God wants you to have money, but does not want money to have you.

Let us look again at 3 John 2: 'Beloved, I wish above all things that thou mayest prosper and be in health, even as thy soul prospereth.' The word 'prosperity,' I admit, has been largely over-used in our day, but that does not undermine its inbuilt meaning as far as the Bible is concerned. Wealth may be associated primarily with money, but when the Scriptures stress that 'God wishes that thou mayest prosper,' it is not limited to money.

The total man

God's plan for your prosperity includes your body, soul and spirit, or, you might say, the total man. That is what the Lord has in mind for you, all-out prosperity for all areas of your life. Hallelujah! My beloved friend, you need prosperity in your marriage, your education, your family, your ministry and everything you lay hands on to do.

Let us look at what God told Joshua in chapter one, verse 17 of that book: 'This book of the law shall not depart out of thy mouth . . . for then thou shalt make thy way prosperous . . .' Is that not marvellous? God specifically assured Joshua '. . . make thy way prosperous . . . .' God was not saying that the way in which Joshua would walk every morning would be a smooth or easy path. He meant that in the *way of life* Joshua would prosper. The way of life has many facets, including marriage, children, education, business pursuits and more.

I want to examine in greater detail some key words which we are frequently coming across in this book—basic words or concepts such as 'prosper, prosperity, prosperous,' and 'abound, abundant, abundance.' We are not indulging in semantics; rather this word study will bring us to a clear position on what prosperity should actually stand for in the Bible.

Basically, abundance in any field of endeavour means that the person involved has all he needs and in addition something to spare and share with others. It implies, essentially, that God has lifted you above the level of your own needs, and thus you are able to reach out to the needs of others.

Success will light your path

The word 'prosper,' particularly as it is used in the Bible, has a sharp connotation of success. In other words, when God talks of prosperity, the indirect connotation is that success will light your path.

It is therefore easy to see from 3 John 2 that prosperity as God directs it to you covers all three areas of life—spiritual, physical and material. In every one of them the supreme will of God is established—to succeed!

Thank God for the freedom we have obtained as a result of enlightenment from His Word, integrated into our lives by faith.

Many years ago when I was growing up in the city of Benin, lifestyle and society generally were not as we see them today. I am not talking about the social infrastructure and development that modernisation has brought to the ancient city of Benin. I am not thinking about the masterpieces of architectural structures which stand imposingly all over our university campuses. My eye is not set on the European-dressed young men and women who occupy places of prominence and power in the corridors of administration in our cities. Deep down in my mind I recollect with nostalgia the days of many years ago when my country was under colonial rule.

Much water has passed under the bridge during the past few decades. The mules have gone. Boreholes are a rare sight; mud-and-thatched buildings are a thing of the past in the city. The grotesque statues which stood at every junction have been swept away by environmental sanitation moves. Dotted all across the wide streets are beautiful architectural works of modern-day building engineers. Times have changed.

As a young boy my curiosity always got the best of me. My little friends and I roamed up and down for fun or mischief. Our wanderings occasionally brought us to the Government Residential Area (G.R.A.), the domain of whites. The G.R.A. was strictly a prohibited area where white colonial administrators lived with their families, a place of beauty and splendour. As we walked between the bungalows I remarked, 'One day I shall live in the G.R.A.' My friends found my statement funny and over-ambitious, but their comments did not disturb my commitment. Time and again as we visited the G.R.A. I surveyed the flowery beauty and the iron gates which surrounded these posh buildings, and I always asserted to my sceptical school-friends: 'Nothing will stop me from living in the G.R.A. one day.'

Many years have come and gone. I did not envisage how I would accomplish the feat of the G.R.A. occupation, but as I laboured for God He began to effect the change I spoke about as a boy.

7

RELIGION OR CHRISTIANITY?

With God all things are possible.
Matthew 19.26

There is no doubt that the men of the Early Church, as shown in the Acts of the Apostles—or 'Acts of the Holy Spirit'—were men who knew what they were about. Sometimes detractors have called that primitive Christianity, but I opt for all that.

As an apostle by the grace of God in this generation, I have seen enough in my ministry to distinguish between religion and Bible-faith or full-Gospel Christianity.

God had a purpose in raising me in Benin City, once known as the city of blood. Today, through the power of the Cross, Benin is acclaimed a stronghold of modern-day revival and of course the city of Jesus Christ. I have lived here long enough to know what dead religion and idolatry can do to a people. But praise be to God in the highest, over the years I have seen Bible-faith Christianity topple religion and heathenism.

My friend, read this chapter with an open heart and total surrender to the Holy Spirit that in the choice set before you, whatever it takes, you will believe God for change.

Why preach healing?

Let me share this with you. Press interviews are a common trial in my trips around the world proclaiming Christ and Him crucified. Common questions that mass media practitioners often ask me include, 'How do you heal?', 'Why do you preach healing?', and 'Why don't some of the older churches preach miracles?' Frankly, these questions have often aroused my deepest reasoning about religion and full-Gospel Christianity.

The same questions are asked in Australia, the United States of America, and Asia; and recently in Maiduguri in Northern Nigeria the press had good reason to ask them. Unbelievers may be in darkness, but they have light enough in their minds to differentiate between dead-end religion and Holy Ghost-empowered ministry.

Years ago when I stood at the edge of a sin-filled, idol-ridden, religion-torn city, I cried to God, 'Father, I desire something better than this.' My yearning heart could not be satisfied by ritual, bazaars and picnics; I sought to see the power of Elijah's God. The indifference, the solemn assembly of the religious institutions, and the lack of spiritual power, left painful beats in my bosom. Here and there dim lights shone, but worldly conformity had spread over the religious houses; they offered nothing but vain amusements and I could hear the lamentation, even as Jeremiah cried, 'How is the gold become dim!'

God gave me a heavenly burden and I chose to change. It is my prayer that the same challenges and burdens would be released in your soul, even *now*!

Step on to new ground

Choose to change! Look over your city, town or village and cry out to God for its redemption. The great Scottish revivalist prayed and wept many days, 'Father, give me Scotland or I die!' Is that your cry? Step out of the crowd and receive the anointing for change, to change others. Step out of religion and enter the blazing light of liberty and miracles.

As you vow to change and pledge to step on to new ground, I believe the Lord God will say to you as He did to me years ago: 'Go through the midst of the city, through the midst of Jerusalem, and set a mark upon the foreheads of the men that sigh and that cry for all the abominations that be done in the midst thereof.' Even as these words register in your heart, be pressed in your spirit and bear the cross, counting the reproach of Christ greater riches than all the treasures of Egypt.

My challenge to you is clear and resounding. It is a Gospel challenge! Don't sit down and allow the truth of God to be trodden as mire in the street. May the Lord look down on you today and see your burdened spirit as a sincere token of true love to Him; those who love the Lord Jesus are wounded in His woundings and vexed with the vexings of His spirit. Take a stand for the God of miracles. I did, and saw His power sweep across Benin City.

Christianity is supernatural

My discovery is going to be your discovery. If we do not have the supernatural in Christianity, we have nothing to offer the heathen but a religion, and true Christianity is not a religion. Religion is only a form, a ceremonial observance, but Christianity is a life in itself. Christianity is the core, heart and nature of Jesus Christ being manifested in man. Praise the Lord, Christianity is the miracle-life. It began in miracles; we can declare it is based on a succession of miracles; and even in our day it is propagated by miracles.

The Bible itself is undoubtedly a miracle Book, and that is why we must stake our lives and ministries on nothing but that. Man wants a living God!

Dr T. L. Osborn and his wife Daisy, of the United States of America, have been a mighty influence on us to the glory of God. In some of their tapes and in one of their numerous books, the Osborns share an interesting and dynamic testimony which proved a turning point in their great ministry. They married in their early youth and had considerable zeal for God's work and a heartfelt burden for lost souls. In search of missionary exploits, they journeyed down to Asia and pitched their Gospel tent in India. Before long, what they feared confronted them; the Moslems among whom they were evangelising opposed them vehemently. 'If, as you say, the Jesus Christ of the Bible died and rose, let Him prove Himself and we would believe the Gospel you preach,' the ridiculing and incredulous Moslems told the Osborns everywhere they went.

The Osborns were caught mid-stream, seemingly helpless in the circumstances. They looked at the

Moslem Koran as it lay near their Bible. The Bible had a black leather covering and so had the Koran. The words in both were printed in black letters. 'Our Koran has silver lining the edge, much like your Bible—what is so special about it?' the Moslems taunted and joked.

The Osborns took what seemed to be the most advisable step out of the crisis—they returned to America. They consoled themselves, 'Well, back home people may believe the Bible without seeking for any sign or manifestation of a living Christ.' But they knew that running away from the problem would not solve it. 'We must seek God, we must go back and prove to the Indians that the Jesus Christ we serve is alive,' they resolved, and as they cried to God they found the answer.

Not long afterwards the Osborns returned to India, to the same city where they had previously met their Waterloo—and glory be to God, Jesus Christ showed Himself alive by many infallible proofs.

Return to Bible teaching

If we return to Bible preaching, we will get Bible results, not religious ceremonies. Christ is as much a miracle worker now as He ever was. You have need of the miracle touch of Jesus Christ now!

The Osborns shared the secret with myself and Margaret, the secret which made me stand and declare, 'God, in this city of blood, the blood-stained banner of Jesus Christ shall fly day and night.'

Today, my friend, a choice is placed before you. Do not dodge the issues; believe in the God of miracles. Have faith in the living God, who baptised me with the Holy Ghost and fire to carry the Gospel of the miracle Jesus around the surface of the earth. 'Fear not'—that is what God is saying to you. Kings, chiefs, thrones, powers and men have risen against me for the sake of the Gospel, but look to the word of the Apostle Paul, 'At the end of it all, stand!'

Many years ago, I made my lifetime choice to change and serve the living God. To step into Miracle Centre, Benin City, is to enter the realm of miracles and the very presence of God Almighty. The church building, holding 7,000 people, faces you on the left. A straight walk brings you to the corridors of the international office, displaying a vast array of photographs depicting my more than 25 years of miracle ministry by the grace of God. On the far right of the large campus stands the Jesus People Faith Building of the All Nations for Christ Bible Institute, with students from every continent. A dome-shaped building houses our internationally-recognised PTL and Idahosa World Outreach television ministry, capable of seating over 2,000 in a lecture session. Facing this is the Prayer House. The Evangelism House is the home of our foreign missionaries labouring for the Kingdom.

Just a few minutes' drive would bring you to what will soon become the City of Faith. The Word of Faith Schools (kindergarten and college) stand face to face. The incredible Arena of Faith, a 30,000-seater cathredrome, stands over and above every building in the vicinity.

Why need I share all these achievements which God has brought to pass in my ministry? The reason is simple. Men and women said, 'It is impossible, it cannot be done.' But I listened to the voice of God and said, 'I choose to change, for with God nothing shall be impossible.'

God is speaking to you now. Please step out of the crowd. Make a choice, one that leads to the path of success, victory and glory to our God on high!

8

LIVING IN GOD'S ABUNDANCE

Jesus said . . . 'I am come that they might have life, and that they might have it more abundantly.'

John 10.10

Through the accelerated growth and expansion of my ministry God has taught me some truths which I share with you to bring you to a new place of Christian faith. It is the considered goal of every believer to reach the place of living in God's abundance. Sadly this has been but a mirage and dream for many and I desire to put into your hands the keys to God's plan for abundance.

The society in which we live today makes it almost impossible for a man or woman without a disciplined life to understand, or totally embrace, the truth that Almighty God can and will supply every need. The Bible says to the believer, 'We live in this world but we are not of this world.' In other words, the standards of daily living for a believer in the world are in contrast with those of the unbeliever.

God has been waiting and longing through the ages for people who will obey His voice, accept His challenges, and above all go forth with the Word of life to the world, proving that He can heal and save, as well as provide for the financial needs of His children as they believe Him.

Many years ago I read a word of Scripture which ministered profoundly to me and still rings in my spirit. It is Numbers 14:21: 'But as truly as I live, all the earth shall be filled with the glory of the Lord.' Hallelujah! The earth shall be filled with His glory. The salvation of souls from darkness to the marvellous light of Jesus Christ brings glory to God. The deliverance of the heathen from idolatry and fetishism brings glory to Him. So also financial provision for the children of God brings glory to the Lord our God.

God is going to use you believers, and all those who belong to Him, as His agency to fill the earth with His glory. We will be the dispensers who will be used to fill the face of the earth with the glory of God. I am ready to be used of God to fill the earth with His glory; are you?

Some of you are facing difficulties, hardships, tribulations and various forms of discouragements. The high mountains don't seem to budge even one inch, but be assured that it doesn't matter what the circumstances are like—stand upon the Word. Through the years of ministry I have been faced endlessly with seemingly irresolvable situations, but in every case I looked beyond them to the Word of the Lord. It was only by faith that I saw God prove His abundance.

A God of abundance

God is a God of abundance. That is not an abstract statement; I am a living witness of God's abundance even when men and women have said the contrary. It took me some years to identify the key to God's abundance and on that score I can confidently proclaim, 'Everything He does is big.'

The Christian experience is one of superabundance, beginning with salvation of the soul. Jesus Christ said the thief comes to kill and steal and destroy, but He came to bring abundant life (Jn 10.10). The word 'abundant' has other related meanings including 'sufficiency' and 'plentiful.' It is clear, therefore, that Christ can give you sufficiency and plentiful provision in your day-to-day needs.

The supreme purpose of God's abundant life for you is not just so that you may drive around in a flashy car and have the biggest mansion in town. To the child of God, 'abundance' means much more than these transitory objectives of limited scope. God through Christ gave us light that we might shine. God through the riches of Christ gives us abundance that we might help the needy and hopeless. As you tap into the resources of God, allow the abundance to stream down to those in need.

I find joy in encouraging men and women in the things of God. This is a fundamental reason why I spend time sharing with my congregation, 'The sick cannot help the sick, neither can the blind lead the blind.' Sometimes I tell them, 'The only reason why you must be a rich Christian is so that you may be able to reach out and lift others from the quagmire of filth and squalor.'

Everything our God does is on a grand scale. If you doubt it, take a look at the size of the universe. How far can your eyes go? It is a limitless expanse created by a limitless God.

Provision in the wilderness

The deliverance of the children of Israel from Egypt by Jehovah was an undeniable miracle of vast magnitude, beyond our imagination. It is estimated by Bible scholars and theologians that about 3½ million Jews were involved in God's rescue operation. Some time ago I came across a piece of research material about God's provision in the wilderness and it confounded my mind. The estimate proved that nearly 4,000 tons of manna were needed each day for consumption by the people. That is a staggering figure, if you puzzle out what 4,000 tons means. Surprisingly, God gave the children of Israel each day's provision, according to the Bible account, for 40 years. Try and work out what that amounts to! (Ex 16) Let me help you with the figure. For 40 years, a total of 14,600 days, or 58,400,000 tons of manna. We can also estimate that with all the livestock and people in the massive group, something in the region of 60,000 tons of water would be needed each day.

God is a great God. God is an abundant God, not limited by space or time. The fun of it is that someone said it cost God about 100 billion dollars over 40 years to get the Israelites out of Egypt! Why did God go to such expense to provide for the children of Israel? The reason is simple: they chose to serve the living God and so He put Himself under obligation to prove His abundance in their midst (Jer 33.3).

The logic inherent in this illustrious account is that if the children of Israel had decided to stay in Egypt in direct disobedience to God's commandment, there would have been no need for divine miraculous provision. The lesson is simple for your understanding; if you come out of Egypt, you shift responsibility to God. If you choose to change, God chooses to stand by you.

My friend, let us settle this point. Failure to comprehend the Kingdom principles of God results in stagnation. Just as the Israelites did, you can call upon Him to supply you out of His abundance. You can say, 'Abba, Father.' Say with me, 'I am a Kingdom child and I have Kingdom rights to possess Kingdom abundance and provisions.'

Get involved in the Word; do not perish for lack of knowledge (Hos 4.6). Get in perfect tune with God and lay hold on your possessions.

Archbishop Benson Idahosa

with Kenneth and Gloria Copeland

The Faith Miracle Centre

and the Word of Faith School

The Archbishop on crusade

9

GIVING AND RECEIVING

My God will supply all your need according to His riches in glory by Christ Jesus.

Philippians 4.19

The living God stands behind the living Word. That should sound logical to your ears. We are witnesses to millions of promises and contracts that men have not been able to honour. In most cases, the parties involved in the promise or contract proved dishonest or insincere and therefore could not uphold their word. Circumstances, crises and upheavals abound in the world, and such catastrophes and disasters to a large extent leave in their wake death and destruction, with untold effects on human arrangements and endeavours. Promises are sometimes altered by natural disasters, which are beyond human control and influence.

It is therefore possible to establish the premise that with the best of intentions man may not be able to keep a promise because of factors beyond his control. But we cannot and dare not say that of God. God has declared He will hasten His Word to perform it (Jer 1.12), and He has also stressed that His Word will not return void (Is 55.11). God is not a man that He will lie (Rom 3.4). Unlike man, God makes a promise and ensures its fulfilment. Abraham knew this truth long ago, 'being fully persuaded that what he had promised he was able also to perform' (Rom 4.21).

One of the most painful duties for many Christians is giving to God. You will have to sit in my school through the lessons I want to share here, and make a change for good. It takes time to reach financial maturity. A lesson I learned many years ago is that financial bondage or stagnation is the direct result of trusting in ourselves and not sticking to the promises of God.

As our ministry expanded, so did our commitment and daily expenditure. The budget was bulging and breaking at the seams. It was at this point that God gave me an unusual revelation about giving. I was a bit scared.

Letters were pouring in from every nation of the world. All manner of needs came to us. Gradually other developing ministries began to depend on us for more than counsel—they needed financial support. Our crusades in countries far and near increased the intake of foreign scholarship awards, and that meant a need for more finances, while on the home front our projects accelerated beyond budget estimates, and we all knew the hour for divine intervention with finances had come.

Hundreds of people call on us at home from America, Europe, African nations and other states of Nigeria. I could not break my policy of 'Eat before you go.' I was proud to be able to say, 'In my house

God sets a table in the presence of my friends.'

But here I stood, hemmed in beyond escape by ministerial demands, at home, in the office and from abroad. At an awkward time such as this I heard the voice of God clearly—'My son Idahosa, prove Me with 90% tithe and I will show you great and mighty things you know not of.'

A test of faith

I could not believe my ears. It stunned me. It was a test of faith, unequal to any other I had encountered. 'How do I give 90% tithe to God at a time such as this? Could this be the voice of God?' I asked myself in astonishment. After much self-inspired debate I assured myself, 'Well, the devil would certainly not tell a believer to give 90% to God's work!'

Acting on a demand as stretching as this takes much re-examination and re-assertion. It is not due to lack of faith in believing God, but the human side of man wrestling and the devil working overtime to dissuade you. Then out of the stalemate, God took my mind to Romans 4.21. God's Word is irrevocable and I needed no other confirmation. But I had one more hurdle to overcome—my wife. How should I share such a demanding request with her?

'Honey, I have something important to share with you from God,' I said pensively after our morning family worship. She asked me cheerfully, 'What is the good news? Can you tell me now?'

I said, 'Honey, God spoke to me about two nights ago, that we should give 90% tithe to His work.'

'What did you say, please?' she asked incredulously, out of anxiety rather than from lack of hearing.

I repeated the statement to her and an unusual silence took over. She tightened her grip of the chair and solemnly bowed her head. With calculated gentleness she looked up into my face and said with great emphasis, 'You mean God wants to kill us—we could as well give all and starve.'

Now I knew I had heard from God, which is the most crucial dimension in any step of faith. We must look to God as the source of our needs. Whenever we take our eyes off God and His will for our life, we immediately begin to attempt to do things our own way. Far too often, our way is to look at the future, the task; figure out how much our budget can stand in payments; and go and borrow the money.

Obedience counts

Dear Christian friend, as God works to bring us to financial maturity, He cannot demonstrate His power to supply our needs if we don't let Him. Obedience counts. Sometimes, too, the opportunity of God's provision is missed because many try to do it ahead of His schedule and miss a blessing from Him.

You are probably itching to hear what came of the 90% tithing to God's work. After much prayer and determination I embarked on giving 90% of all my earnings to God's work. That called for absolute faithfulness on my part. Day by day and month by month, as I began to see God's miraculous provisions in various areas of the ministry, it dawned on me, 'God is faithful to the utmost!'

In this momentous journey of faith regarding the 90% tithing I learned some life-transforming lessons. God gives and takes. I realised that if He demands 90% tithe, then He puts Himself under obligation to provide enough for me to live comfortably on the remaining ten per cent. The Gospel truth is that God's remaining ten per cent was more than enough. Hallelujah!

On the other hand, I observed that financial responsibility is two-fold. First, it involves our responsibility to God, and secondly God's responsibility to us. We all know there is no problem with God's side of the contract because His Word is forever settled in heaven. The problem is with man. Only when we demonstrate to God our avowed maturity in financial matters can He demonstrate His power to supply our every need.

Basic principles

God has taught me enough about financial maturity to know that it involves these three basic principles:

1. *Giving*: To God; Christians; the poor—Malachi 3.10; Romans 12.13; Proverbs 19.17.
2. *Receiving*: From answered prayer; fruitful labour; God-given talents—Romans 12.11; Proverbs 31.
3. *Spending*: Best buy; buying according to finances, not speculation.

I choose to change from stinginess to being a fruitful giver by obedience to God's Word. I understand, 'God shall supply . . .' (Phil 4.19a). That Scripture does not say the government, your trade union organisation or your employer shall supply. God is your supply; if you miss that, you miss everything else. God does not change as governments come and go. He is not fickle-minded as some employers are who give you a raw deal through underpayment. I choose to change from trusting man for my finances. God is my supply. Whoever your employer is or whatever job you handle, do it unto the Lord and receive His reward (check Colossians 3.22–23).

One of the early truths I discovered as a believer was that I was entitled to some blessings from the throne of God. I found out that the Christian life is one of multiplication, it is not static.

We are begotten of God through Christ. Our lives are hid with Christ in God. It stands to reason on this account that everything we ever need comes from God the Father through Jesus, the one and only source.

Take a look at 2 Peter 1.3: 'According as his divine power hath given unto us all things that pertain unto life and godliness, through the knowledge of him that hath called us to glory and virtue.' The Apostle who wrote this epistle uses the past tense, rather than a future tense. The understanding therefore is, God has already given us all we are going to need for time and evermore.

Choose to change today. Change your prayer pattern with this fresh revelation that God has already given us all we need in this life. Christians often pray vain repetitive prayers based on sheer misunderstanding. God's provision is enclosed in promises. Provision is in the promise. Learning this fact has done me much good in claiming my Kingdom blessings.

Our inheritance

Secondly, I discovered that God's promises are our

inheritance. They are *your* inheritance through Christ. When you come to Christ you become an heir of God and joint-heir with Jesus Christ. In other words, the whole inheritance is yours with legal backing. I hope you will understand that you can own much legally, but enjoy little in actual experience. This is very much like being the son of a millionaire king who does not know who his father is. The day he finds out, everything falls into place. But until he finds out, he still is the son of a millionaire king, by legal entitlement as a son.

Thirdly, change your conception and thinking with this Scriptural truth. All the promises of God are a solid expression of His will for His children in Christ. Can you imagine God promising something He cannot do, or anything that is not His will?

Jesus Christ made a revealing statement in Luke 11.13: 'If ye then, being evil, know how to give good gifts unto your children, how much more shall your heavenly Father give . . .' God Himself loves to give us His best, and we ought to know this, way down in our hearts (Rom 8.31).

You don't need all of God's promises right here and now. The fact is, it is impossible to claim all God's promises in one split second, but any promise you need that fits your situation is available to you now!

From all I have been setting out here let me summarise the principles precisely for your benefit:

1. His provisions are in His promise.
2. His promises are in our inheritance.
3. His promises are an exact expression of His will.

4. His promises are available to us now through Christ.
5. The fulfilment of His promises for us does not depend upon our circumstances, but rather upon our meeting His conditions.

I choose to change with these principles, and I assure you that as you take these steps, His promise and provision will become real to you.

10

POSITIVE CONFESSION

For with the heart man believeth unto righteousness; and with the mouth confession is made unto salvation.
Romans 10.10

We have all along been talking about taking steps of redirection to possess the abundance and fulfilment of God. In the book of Proverbs you will read a strange word of Scripture which says, 'Thou art ensnared by the words of thy mouth.' The connotation in this verse sounds more negative, but even if it is, I believe there could be a positive side to it.

The Apostle Paul under the inspiration of the Holy Spirit wrote the epistle to the believers in Rome, and in it we have a complete exposition of the central truths of Christianity. Among the great truths Paul wrote were Romans 10.10: 'For with the heart man believeth unto righteousness; and with the mouth confession is made unto salvation.'

Confession comes from the heart through utterance by the mouth. This is why you must learn from today to confess things and speak words that will uplift, edify and bless you. Negative thoughts lead to negative confession, which ends up in fear, doubt and failure. In the same manner, positive, sound and Scriptural thoughts result in faith-full confession leading to assurance, promise and hope in God.

Men everywhere want to succeed. But to many success is an illusion. The Bible tells us that God's wish is for every man and woman in Christ to rise to life's highest point of success and achievement. This brings glory to His Name.

Although many desire to be rich, a familiar story of failure and unfulfilment is written in many lives. The vital question is, 'Why is it that some people are happier than others, some richer than others and some more blessed than others?' The Scripture says, 'God is no respecter of persons.' What God has done for one He is well able to do for another. In the light of these questions let us determine the contributing factor in the differences in people's ways of life, making some happier, richer, more fulfilled and more successful than others.

The Bible, God's authentic and reliable Word, has answers to what by human standards are seemingly insoluble problems.

Let us consider a couple of Scriptures and see how they relate to our study and how best we can effectively apply and live by these principles. First, Mark 11.13–14: 'And seeing a fig tree having leaves he came if haply he might find anything thereon: and when he came to it he found nothing but leaves, for the time of figs was not yet. And Jesus answered and said unto it, No man eat fruit of thee hereafter for ever. And his disciples heard it.'

There is a secret here you must know. Do you know that the tree did not speak, but the life of the tree, its action and characteristics spoke for it? There is a great lesson to learn here. Your way of life, how you live and conduct your life, determines to a great extent your success or failure. Jesus Christ came to the tree expecting to find fruit, but there was none. And so He spoke to the tree, 'No man eat fruit of thee hereafter for ever.' The Bible narrates that the following day Peter remembered and recognised that the tree was dead. Peter recollected the words spoken by Jesus on the previous day, particularly the curse on the tree when Jesus had found it served no purpose to humanity.

Importance of words

You can speak life or death to your dreams and visions. That is why it is very important to study and watch carefully the word that proceeds out of your mouth, because God watches over it to bring it to pass.

My point is, if the tree died because Jesus spoke and cursed it for not bearing fruit, then we as Christians must also speak and expect mighty big results. God speaks and expects results. And we are made in the image and likeness of Him.

There are many people today who cannot speak to their circumstances because the devil continues to generate negative confessions out of their mouths. You are the speaker, God is the doer. Therefore do not let your dreams die halfway. Do not let your visions die midstream. Do not reduce the scope of your thoughts and what you can achieve in life. God never gives up on His dream. You must not!

Secondly, Genesis 1.1–2: 'In the beginning God created the heaven and the earth. And the earth was without form and void, and darkness was upon the face of the deep.' After the creation of the world, the Bible says, it was formless and void and very dark. There was no growth and therefore no progress. But when God spoke, the Spirit of God moved into action and things started to happen.

'And God said, Let there be light, and there was light.' The first thing God does for you in conversion is to take your darkness and give you light. The power of light destroys and fills the vacuum left in you.

You see, God created all things in suspense, on a standby basis. The sea was created and put into an inactive state. So were fishes, trees, light and everything else. They did not take their respective and proper positions till God said, 'You light be there, and you mountains stand here, you settle here.' Everything you desire on earth is standing by for you. But it will never materialise while you are hoping, guessing and thinking. Do you think when God said 'Let there be birds' then fish began to fly? No! There was the creative time before the spoken word. God created the world, but in a state of void. It was not until God spoke that the things created began to fit into their respective places. Your visions and dreams of what you want to be will not materialise until you speak them. Speak to your visions and dreams and bring them to fruition.

You dream and see yourself flying to London. Fine. When you wake up from the dream you are where you are. Get up from your dream, go on your knees and say, 'Lord, next week I am going to London.' It is the same with sickness. If you dream that you are sick, do you claim the sickness for yourself? No. When you get up from such a dream quickly kneel down and curse that foul spirit of sickness, reject it before it really happens to you, saying, 'I curse you in the name of Jesus.' Do you wait until you are sick before you say, 'Oh! I really dreamt that I was sick.' Listen!—the other thing is that when God made the world He put only two people in the vast world. As far as God is concerned, your time and the places due you on this earth are limitless. If you are in business, you are not limited to trade only in your own town. You can expand your scope over the whole surface of the world. God is not going to say, 'Because I made you and put you here you must limit yourself to being here.'

It is the same thing if you are a pastor. Your home town is your Jerusalem; the world is your parish. The commission is to 'go into all the world.' This is the only time and opportunity you have in all your life to subdue and dominate the world. Have dominion in this world. Be fruitful—not in another world; multiply and dominate the world, increase, not in another world but right here. The power to subdue and dominate will be taken away from you when Jesus comes. The will of God is for you to succeed. How? God made the world and it had no form and was void. God did not fold His hands and wait to see the world rot away. Many of you are allowing your dreams and visions to rot away in your heads. God was not satisfied with the state of the world. The Bible says, 'And God said.' Speak to your dreams and visions and bring them to reality.

Let the contents of your heart proceed from your mouth. When it proceeds watch it and put 'Amen' to it. It is to the extent of the scope of your understanding of God that your business is limited. Your dream and vision is in God's hand.

You must speak

God spoke and there was light. God spoke and there were fish. God spoke and the fowls of the air came into existence. God spoke and things came into being. God has already spoken that you are going to be somebody in life (3 Jn 2). You must speak what God has already ordained you to be and it will come to pass. Change it from dream to reality. Turn excuses to uses. Turn your inabilities to God's ability. Then God will fulfil your heart's desire (Mk 11.24).

When God spoke, everything He said came to pass. Then Jesus came and did as the Father had done. Jesus spoke (as a Levite qualified to preach) and said, 'The Kingdom of God is at hand.'

Christ came to turn your life from slavery into Kingdomhood. The Bible says we are now Kingdom children. And as Kingdom children we must speak and bring to pass our heart's desire.

Jesus said in Mark 11.22–24: 'Whosoever shall say unto this mountain . . .' That's where you come in. God is a speaker and you must be a speaker; Jesus spoke to all situations in life and everything that Christ spoke to obeyed. When He spoke to the dumb, the dumb spirit left. When Jesus spoke to death, life came to take its place. In everything that Jesus spoke to, the vacuum of voidness left and the life of fulness came in. The rotten and hopeless state left and life, light, joy and victory came in.

Today it is your turn to speak and God will honour the words of your mouth. Bless yourself. Bless your business, bless your family with what you say, for what you bless on earth is blessed in heaven (Mt 16.19).

God spoke and it came to pass. Jesus spoke and

received results. You can now speak what Jesus has spoken and you will find the same results as Jesus did. You are a Christian. Yes—Christlike. There must be no difference between you and Jesus in your attitude to life. Speak like the Kingdom child you are and see your visions and dreams come to fruition.

Before Jesus there was a man called Moses. We read in Numbers 20.8 that he was told to 'take the rod and gather the assembly together, thou and Aaron thy brother, and speak ye unto the rock before their eyes.' What did God tell Moses to do? To speak to the rock. And what was going to happen? Water was going to come out. In fact until Moses carried out the instruction and spoke, nothing would have happened.

But there are many rocks in your life which need only your speaking to them to release their stored contents. Why has the water not come out? Because you are looking at the rock as a stone, but God is seeing it as a reservoir.

Look at Joshua 10.12: 'Then spake Joshua to the Lord in the day when the Lord delivered the Amorites before the children of Israel.' What are the first words that Joshua spoke? He spoke to the Lord. In the face of the defeat of the enemy Joshua could not hold his peace. He spoke to the Lord and said in the sight of Israel, 'Sun, stand thou still upon Gibeon, and thou moon in the valley of Ajalon.' At whose words did the sun and moon stand still? The words of Joshua, a man like you.

Elijah put 450 priests of Baal to the test. After defeating them he spoke and there was no rain or dew for 42 months. At his word the rain and dew stopped work for three-and-a-half years. What made the sun and moon stop? The word! What caused the rain and dew not to fall? The word! Today, you are the successor of these people. Speak to your dreams, speak to your visions, speak to your heart's desires. Let them come to pass by the authority of the Word of God.

Lord, I bless You for the Word. It is written for our salvation and admonition.
Lord, as I begin to confess Your Word in positive faith, I believe the change I am seeking will dawn.
Lord, You are in your Word to hasten it to performance.
Thank You for the joy of serving You in Christ.

11

LIVING LIKE ABRAHAM

By faith Abraham, when he was called to go out into a place which he should afterwards receive for an inheritance, obeyed, and he went out, not knowing whither he went.

Hebrews 11.8

Salvation is based on the fact that if you truly believe in your heart that God raised Jesus from the dead, and if you confess with your mouth that Jesus is Lord, you will be saved. This interpretation of Scripture is taken from Romans 10.9.

Believing something does not in itself alter its validity or otherwise. The basic difference therefore is to believe something that is true, valid and trustworthy. This is the cornerstone of Christianity; its validity is demonstrated by visible changes in lives, hope for the future and divine intervention to back up the Word.

The God of the Bible is able to say emphatically, 'I am the first and I am the last, and besides me there is no God' (Is 44.6). He is a God in whom to trust and to whom we may look up in every crisis of life. It has been said that a man's belief must be in something superior to himself. On that score a believer in Christ anchors his belief in a God who made all things by His great power.

This is an age of uncertainty, depression and fear. Everywhere there are living corpses, men and women who fear something, not knowing what. In government offices, at stock exchanges, in banks and schools, at the market places, more than ever before men are plagued by fear. For many, hope is lost. Countless millions are looking for refuge in something, provided it can offer a shadow of consolation for a moment of time. All these people believe in something. It may be money; but inflation comes all too soon and depreciation sweeps all hope away. Others put their faith in somebody they have come to trust, but the friendship goes sour and with it go all affiliations and dependence.

I have been talking about belief because we all know that what a man believes in, he also invests his faith in. My belief is in the God of Jesus Christ and therefore my faith is in the Lord.

Let us take one more look at Romans 10.9: 'If thou shalt confess with thy mouth the Lord Jesus, and shalt believe in thine heart that God hath raised Him from the dead, thou shalt be saved.' This is an interesting verse of Scripture which is full of meaning. The last part says, '. . . thou shalt be saved.' Yes, you can know, as well as you know you are alive, that salvation is real. 'Thou shalt be saved!' From what to what? That is a vital question for thought. The Bible declares that Christ the Lord has redeemed us from the curse of the law (Gal 3.13). In other words, Christ has saved us from the curse of the law and brought us to the fulness of the Father through grace.

The church in the dispensation of grace is the consummation of the promise through Abraham. The Bible minces no words, stating, 'God having provided some better thing for us, that they without us should not be made perfect' (Heb 11.40). It is evident that through the work of Christ we have better things (promises) under the New Testament.

My dear friend, let us face facts. You are either in some form of religion or you are serving the living Christ in faith and grace. Which do you belong to?

Limited conception

All over the continent of Africa and in hamlets, villages, towns and cities around the world I have seen believers in hopeless submission to frightening and depressing conditions. They are born-again, Spirit-filled, but restricted by their limited conception of God's prospering power to lift them to new dimensions of blessing and success. There is profound truth in the words of A. B. Simpson, who had good reason to say 'Our God has boundless resources. The only limit is in us. Our expectations are too limited.'

I have always insisted Scripturally that religion leads men to bondage, fear and bleakness, but through Christ, grace and faith lead men to success, prosperity and fulfilment. The Bible says God took man out of the miry clay and placed him on the rock. Religion is nothing but miry clay. God has put you on good ground, solid rock; do not allow manmade traditions, dogmas and regulations to enslave you. 'Stand fast therefore in the liberty wherewith Christ hath made us free, and be not entangled again with the yoke of bondage' (Gal 5.1).

Thank God for the life of the Apostle Paul. He

instructed the Galatian brethren not to return to the miry clay. He used the word again, an indication that the Galatians had once been in a mess and that Christ had delivered them to new life, aspiration, liberty and success.

One of the things that baffles me is the demoralising influence of religion on spiritually blind millions all over the world. Religion offers nothing; it is a dark alley leading nowhere. Early in my ministry I came across a religious sect in one of the neighbourhoods of Nigeria. On 'weekend day' all members of the sect assemble on their church premises. A bugle is sounded after the fashion of Gideon in the Old Testament. They gather in the blazing sun singing and dancing, whilst in one corner young men busy themselves slaughtering sacrificial lambs for the atonement of sin. Space would not allow for the long list of ritualistic practices and orgies these people carry out. As you can see, they are still attached to Old Testament practices, yet plainly the Bible says, 'Christ has redeemed us from the curse of the law' (Gal 3.13).

Elsewhere in Galatians (4.4), we read, 'But when the fulness of time was come, God sent forth his son, made of a woman, made under the law, to redeem them that were under the law . . .' Do you know that Christ has already redeemed us from the curse of the law? Calvary bears the witness. Friends, do you know God's fulness of time has long passed and Christ has already set us free from all forms of religious bondage? Why then is it that men still languish in bondage, unwilling to accept the good news of redemption and liberty? The answer is simple—ignorance and religious trickery have taught a false doctrine which sanctifies poverty and demeans what Christ has esteemed.

Christianity supports the practice of positive faith for God's richest and abundant life. The Bible says, 'The blessing of the Lord it maketh rich and he adds no sorrow with it' (Prov 10.22).

What did the pharisaic ecclesiastical system hand down? Sanctification of poverty—false claims that ordinary people are not qualified to manage material wealth without being destroyed by its inherent malignancy, false claims that prosperity generates pride and sinful living. All these deadly teachings enthroned as religious doctrine ultimately neutralise and kill the believer's drive and creativity and his aspiration to greater heights. So gradually people withdraw and pine away in squalor, depression, insignificance and dejection. But I want to proclaim to you that the good news Jesus Christ came to preach touches the total man, because it is a message of salvation and glory, a message which uplifts.

One day Jesus Christ said to the Pharisees, 'If you were Abraham's children, you would do the things Abraham did.' That was a serious statement and I think they did not even understand what Jesus was talking about. In the first place, they lacked Abraham's faith and therefore could not do the things he did. Jesus challenged the biological descendants of Abraham to live like his spiritual children. It is sad that, even today, many claim the bloodline of Abraham through Christ but do not live like him.

The point Jesus wanted the Pharisees to understand was that as natural descendants of Abraham, they had to do what he had done. Abraham had believed God and all His promises. That is the crux of the matter in our day. Many believe in Christ but not in His promises. How sad! For us today, living in faith simply means putting the full weight of our lives on Jesus and being led by the Holy Spirit to appropriate all the promises.

Abraham made a choice, just as you have to; you are even going to believe God for a change in your situation and circumstances.

Poverty is simply the condition below that of ease and comfortable living—financially, physically and spiritually. Prosperity is success in all areas—spiritual, financial and physical. The good news brings you new revelation and understanding to realise that you can prosper in your marriage, employment, business, education, ministry and anything else.

Life in the Word

One thing I know for sure, God is in His Word, much as life is in the seed. When the seed is planted in the ground, that is, in good ground, it will germinate and grow. When the seed of God's Word is planted in people, it produces its kind. God's Word promises healing, salvation, deliverance and also prosperity.

The Bible is a precious book; it contains nuggets of gold for your life. For many years in my ministry I used a motor-cycle for evangelism, and I valued it highly. As the years passed, the wear and tear of time left my motor-cycle a rickety heap. 'Lord,' I prayed earnestly, 'I need a better means of transportation for the ministry.' In no time the Lord provided me with a new car. I drove it with great relish in massive evangelistic outreach. One day it developed engine trouble and all my desperate efforts to revive it proved fruitless.

'You must call the engineer immediately,' my wife suggested, which I did without delay.

'Please, do you have a manual for the engine?' the engineer enquired after careful examination. 'Manual?' I replied with some hesitation. 'Yes, please get me the engine manual so that I can trace the fault and rectify it,' the engineer insisted. After what proved a rather frantic search I dug up the manual from beneath a stack of discarded books. With a reluctant smile the engineer advised, 'My pastor, keep this engine manual handy; it will save you much trouble!'

Some years ago the Holy Spirit brought to my remembrance those passing words of the engineer, '. . . keep this engine manual handy; it will save you much trouble.' New light was shed on it in my spirit. 'When you were created,' the Holy Spirit revealed, 'a manual for the good of your life was given you, and it is the Bible.' Suddenly it was as though a veil had been drawn back from my mind; I began to nod my head in affirmation. When God created man, in His wisdom, grace and knowledge He added a manual (the Bible) to show us the way to fruitful and successful living. Remember Jesus said, 'I am the way' (Jn 14.6).

Take a look at what God told Joshua (Jos 1.8): 'This book of the law shall not depart out of thy mouth; but thou shalt meditate therein day and night, that thou mayest observe to do according to all that is written therein: for then thou shalt make thy way prosperous, and then thou shalt have good success.' Read this verse again. The Almighty Himself said these words to Joshua—in other words, 'Joshua, if you are going to succeed, better read the manual (the Bible) in which I have carefully set out all the guidelines.'

This generation is one of laxity and carelessness; no wonder many people are not making much headway in life. Go and read the manual (the Bible) and correct the errors in your life; then shall you make your way prosperous. Read the Bible daily, sow the seed of faith and blessings in the Word in your spirit. The miracle seed of God's miracle promises produces miracles in him that believes: 'And this is the confidence that we have in him, that if we ask anything according to his will, he heareth us' (1 Jn 5.14).

New dawn

The call of Abraham was a delicate one. The Bible states in Genesis 12.1, 'Now the Lord had said unto Abram, Get thee out of thy country, and from thy kindred, and from thy father's house, unto a land that I will show thee.' Good old Abraham, the father of faith, did not have any spiritual contemporaries to look up to. No, no mentors! God commanded him to leave the familiar setting. To go where? Hebrews 11.8 tells us, 'By faith Abraham, when he was called to go out into a place which he should afterwards receive for an inheritance, obeyed, and he went out, not knowing whither he went.' Is that not amazing? Abraham left the known for the unknown; he left the known (sight) for the unknown (faith) (Heb 11.1–6).

Our freedom to act upon our desires and to decide and choose the things we believe are good and right for God and for His people, is the open door to success in life.

Centuries ago historians named Africa 'the dark continent,' but I give glory to God that today it is the fountain of worldwide revival. In every country of Africa a torch of revival is burning that will erupt into a blazing flame of gospel fire. Hallelujah! Just two decades back, religion reigned supreme in Nigeria, but today the light of the Gospel of Jesus Christ is creating reverberations in government, university campuses and market places.

A man can influence the destiny of his nation if only he can believe God, believe himself and set out in determination to succeed where others have failed. If only men would turn their stumbling-blocks into stepping-stones, it would make all the difference.

When conditions became tough and unbearable for David, the Bible says he encouraged himself in the Lord. That is what I also did in my rocky times. I understand and believe that 'The Name of the Lord is a strong tower; the righteous runneth into it and is safe' (Prov 18.10).

Sincerely aspire to greater heights and God will grant you grace to succeed. Accept the fact that God placed you on this earth to succeed, 'for in Him we live and move and have our being . . .' (Ac 17.28). Aspiration is of man; inspiration is of God. One is externally generated, the other is internally stimulated. God puts His desires for good into your heart when you have His viewpoint on life and when you follow the awareness of His work in you.

A burden on the heart

God commanded the Gospel to be preached in every nation and among all people (Mk 16.15–18). As the years rolled by, a burden for the Moslem north of 'God's country,' Nigeria, increased in my heart. Stories of gruesome persecutions of Christians were often rampant. Some churches were burnt by Moslem fanatics, who rejected the Gospel with bitter hatred. One day in 1985 I called my crusade coordinator and alerted him: 'Ron, God has laid a heavy burden on my heart for us to take the Gospel of Jesus Christ to the Moslem north.'

My crusade coordinator sat opposite to me with his mouth open for many minutes. I knew he was calculating the cost and effect. Then, 'Where in the north do we go, and when?', Reverend Ron Childs asked me calmly, his eyes lit with renewed readiness.

Both of us walked to the wall where there was a large map of Nigeria. 'This is where we are going—Maiduguri, the capital of Borno State,' I stated, picking out the spot with a pencil.

Coming together is a beginning, keeping together is progress, working together is success. I knelt down with my crusade coordinator as we prayed and agreed for breakthrough in Maiduguri, a boiling pot of Islamic divisions. At the door I said to him, 'Ron, believe God with me, the power of Jesus Christ will silence once and for all the Islamic upsurge in Maiduguri.' 'Amen,' Ron said, and slipped out with a wave of victory.

This was one crusade I shall never forget. Maiduguri is a tough place. Some people considered the crusade a suicide attempt for my ministry. 'Nobody has succeeded in holding a big crusade in Maiduguri,' a few mainline Christians said in fear. But I know whom I have believed and He will always glorify His Name.

Soon we had the crusade permit from the state government and a sports centre was set aside for our meeting. We were ready for the battle, and sure enough we had a few more surprises. Crusade posters put up by the Idahosa World Outreach were ripped off the walls. Our banners were stolen in the night by saboteurs. Moslem fanatics angrily tore up our crusade handbills.

The most painful experience was the resistance; open and clandestine schemes of a nominally Christian organisation to undermine the crusade effort. You would be shocked to know this Christian organisation spent money on television advertisements disassociating itself from the crusade and, worse still, calling on people to stay away because they did not believe in healing miracles. Friend, the harder the enemy fights you, the harder you must fight to succeed. We accepted all these hurdles as marks of good fortune; sure enough the devil had something he was fighting to protect and I was determined to go for it in Jesus' Name (Lk 10.19).

When the Apostle Paul came to Corinth God gave him assurance. 'Then spake the Lord to Paul in the night by a vision, Be not afraid, but speak, and hold not thy peace; for I am with thee, and no man shall set on thee to hurt thee; for I have much people in this city' (Ac 18.9, 10). God gave me a similar message concerning Maiduguri: 'My son Idahosa, be bold to preach my Word. I shall honour the Word with mighty fruits, for I have much people in this city.' My heart leaped with overflowing delight as I shared with my wife Margaret, 'God is going to do exceeding great works in Maiduguri.'

The ministry is not for wool-gatherers and religious sightseers; you will succeed only by determination in grace. The remarkable success of the Maiduguri Crusade is a sure indication of the new dimensions of faith I appropriated in Christ. A few interesting events took place in that crusade which you would love to read. Do you know God has a good sense of humour? Yes, He has!

I am reminded of the words of William Cowper, the 18th century poet: 'God moves in a mysterious way His wonders to perform.' Oh, what a beautifully refreshing portrayal in words of His great deeds in all the earth. Signs, wonders and spectacular miracles were wrought by the finger of God in this Moslem stronghold. The tens of thousands who swarmed the crusade ground every night upset the forecasts of religious observers. This was not a surprise to me—I am used to crowds everywhere, anywhere.

Lo and behold, the first healing miracle testimony I received was that of a daughter of a leader of the Christian organisation which placed television announcements calling for a boycott of the crusade. Yes, God has a good sense of humour, and above all, no man can stop His movements.

At the end of our crusade, over 200 men and women expressed interest in attending Bible school. I offered 24 full scholarships to indigenes of Borno State for the 1986 session. Many had to be turned away due to lack of space and finances.

To the glory of God, in the full glare of the sceptics and doubting Christians, about 300 converted Moslems and atheists were baptised into the Body of Christ. Today the local Kanuris, Ciboks, Margis, Hausas and Shuwa-Arabs make up a vibrant assembly of believers in the Moslem city of Maiduguri.

My friend, I choose to change. You can also opt for success in your ministry, home or occupation. The greatest triumph in your life is for you to discover yourself in Christ—then to let Him fully develop that unlimited new life of power in you. You can make it! Do not listen to the doubters. Believe the God in you! Believers don't make resolutions, they act with determination. Act in faith; step out in faith and walk on in faith, for there is no other way—the just shall live by faith (Rom 1.12b).

12

SUCCESS ANYWHERE

Have faith in God.

Mark 11.22

Glorious results can only be produced when your actions are based on God's plan, His ideas and certainly His dreams for your life. Divine decisions are followed by divine directions. Desire God's best just where you are, but bear in mind you can never be bigger than your dreams. Therefore *dream big*! Your greatest personal development is to get God's view of the world, to see eye to eye with God and go on hand in hand with Him into a great future of blessing and success.

Early in my ministry I travelled long distances on my motor-cycle to villages in the Bendel State of Nigeria, proclaiming the Gospel and the power of God. In several places only a handful of people assembled, but praise God, this did not affect my anointing and faith. In a few years I moved to the towns to carry on evangelistic outreach on a bigger scale. Gradually the crowds increased.

The need for evangelistic materials reached desperate levels. I wrote to Dr T. L. Osborn of Tulsa, Oklahoma, asking him to send me tracts in large quantities. I had read some of his writings and was fascinated.

In those days America was millions of miles from me and I had no ambition to visit that country. I knew there was a job at home to be accomplished at all costs. There was no doubt in my spirit that God had called me as a national preacher right from the beginning. Years of despair, toil and subsistence level existence had characterised the early years of my ministry. Success was coming, but I was itching for greater exploits day by day.

The national character of my ministry began to blossom and shape. The national newspapers began to recognise it, the days of considering it 'no-news' were over. Testimonies of fantastic healing miracles and mass conversions were reported on the radio and in the newspapers. A new day was emerging. This was in the early seventies.

One singular event took place in my life and ministry which had a remarkable impact and effect on my faith for success. The short spell in Christ for the Nations, Dallas, U.S.A., in 1972 opened my eyes to new vistas of faith and ministry. I was ready to launch into the deep for a bumper harvest of souls. In just a couple of years a deep and lasting relationship between my family and the Osborns (Drs T. L. and Daisy Osborn) was established.

I have already told of my gratitude and appreciation for the spiritual influence of the Osborns upon my ministry. They mean everything to my family and little wonder I named one of my daughters 'Daisy,' after that precious woman of God, the wife of Dr T. L. Osborn. The Osborns took us into their confidence, sharing secrets of apostolic evangelism and ministry with us. In November 1975 we accepted an invitation to visit them in Tulsa. It was a history-making visit. More than that, it was a life-changing journey in my adventure in faith. Above all, it was a mission which helped to prove God beyond measure.

It was a fabulous experience to be special guests of the Osborns. We were overwhelmed by the goodness of God upon them, a remarkable evidence of honour and reward for faithful service in His kingdom. Great opportunities and new doors of enriching ministry were thrown open before us by courtesy of the Osborns. Preaching appointments flooded my desk from far and near in the United States. A new era of fruitful ministry stood before us like an open door. It was a challenge and a bait!

An important issue

During our couple of weeks stay in the United States, Dr Osborn tapped on my door to discuss a very crucial issue with me. 'Dear Benson,' he said, 'I have a rather important issue to discuss with you.'

I ushered him to a sofa in the corner. 'What is it, Brother Osborn?', I enquired, smiling into his ever-cheerful face.

'Benson,' he began, 'I want you to consider the offer of ministerial appointment here in the U.S.A.' I readjusted my position on the sofa as he continued, 'You will be offered not less than fifteen hundred dollars a month for pastoral duties.'

I was so overwhelmed by the proposition that I momentarily lost my power of speech. I sat there staring at Dr Osborn, who gripped my hands understandingly.

Then the Osborns took us both for a ride through the sprawling city. Down the smooth, well-kept road we drove in gorgeous relaxation. As we negotiated a curve, Dr Osborn reiterated lovingly, 'My dear Benson, you are most welcome to live here with us if you so desire; be free to think about it with Margaret.'

The neat mown lawns and beautiful setting of the city as we sped by arrested my attention. Under my breath I sighed, 'A city of splendour and glamour, a dream child of my ambition.' Back from the ride, an unusual uneasiness gripped me. Dr Osborn's attractive proposition did not put me at ease. I invited Margaret to help me examine the full spectrum of this great offer. 'This is a dream come true,' she exclaimed delightedly. 'Honey, with your growing anointed ministry, we can believe God for new horizons of exploits for the Kingdom here in America.'

My mind was crowded. I was standing at the crossroads. No decision had tested my faith like this new development, and of course I knew the implications. My thoughts reeled back to Benin City, Nigeria. The contrast was sharp and vivid. An emerging ministry there was going through deep-seated trials. In the background was the city of blood (Benin) yielding easily to the Gospel. Everything at home pointed to a promising ministry, but down in my heart I knew it was going to be a long way to victory.

Suddenly I thought of the meagre salary I was receiving in Nigeria as pastor-evangelist—the equivalent of fifteen U.S. dollars a month. What was fifteen dollars in Nigeria compared to fifteen hundred a month in the U.S.?

The time for fervent prayers had come; I did not need anyone to tell me that. I called Margaret. 'Honey, please let us seek the face of the Lord on this crucial issue. I want us to walk in the perfect will of God, whatever the cost.'

Together in earnest fellowship we called upon the Lord for His divine directions. I went to bed with mixed feelings. I was divided on the issue. Subject to divine over-ruling of our decision, I intended to go along with Dr Osborn's offer—or so I thought! We went to bed in high spirits.

Right on the dot of midnight I felt someone touch me. I went down on my knees in agonising prayer. The presence of the Lord was evident in that room. My wife was in a deep sleep. The Lord spoke clearly to me. He left me in no doubt concerning what He wanted to communicate to me. There is no room for guesswork with God—His words are straight and emphatic.

The Lord said insistently, 'Benson, go back to Nigeria. That is where I called you from. If you stay in America I will kill you.'

In a twinkle of an eye I saw the dream fizzle out into thin air, and there I lay before the Lord on the floor. What seemed a chance of a lifetime evaporated before my eyes. Fear seized me and there was no more strength left. In a momentary meditation I gently said, 'O Lord God, why, why?'

'Go back'

Then in the haziness of my mind I heard the voice of God saying words I shall never forget all the days of my life—words that have changed my life, my vision and above all my ministry. God said, 'My dear son

Benson, go back to Africa. I called you as my vessel from there to the rest of the world. Whatsoever things you desire, as long as you preach my Word of salvation, healing and power, I shall provide all. Go back *now*!'

After a prayer of thanks I bounced to my feet with renewed vigour and strength. I buttoned up my shirt and headed for Dr Osborn's apartment. The clock sounded 2.00 am. I knocked firmly and when Dr Osborn came to the door I said calmly to him, 'Please, Dr Osborn, God spoke to me—I cannot accept the offer; I must go back home.' For moments not one more word was uttered between us. Then with a deep, sincere smile Dr Osborn placed his hands on my shoulder and assured me, 'Thank you, Benson; goodnight and God bless you.' Great men of God honour His Word!

Before long Margaret and I were on a plane back to Nigeria. We have seen rough and bitter moments since then. There have been times when there did not seem to be any light at the end of the tunnel, but the words of Jesus reassured me, 'Have faith in God' (Mk 11.22).

With divine precision the Almighty God has blessed us beyond measure in the ministry. I have witnessed overwhelming growth and in my family God's Word has come true: 'The blessing of the Lord maketh rich and He addeth no sorrow with it.'

Beloved friend, do not look on the prevailing circumstances, but stand upon what God has said.

13

MASTER KEY TO SUCCESS

The Lord your God has set the land before you: go up and possess it.
Deuteronomy 1.21

More often than not, I tend to think, prosperity and success for a child of God is based on *faith* and *hard work*. Every single thing Jesus did and said was beyond doubt to lift and inspire people. My heart aches with pain when I see Christians who do not believe in hard work.

Jesus Christ, the author and finisher of our faith, believed in hard work. He woke up at night to pray to the Father. Jesus Christ was always in tune with heaven, and when the day broke victory had already been won whilst the world was asleep.

Many times I have had people confront me with this question: 'Archbishop, how do you cope with these gigantic projects and this extensive ministry?' I simply smile! Some eager few go on to ask again, 'Sir, how do you stand being president of a ministry with over 3,000 branches in several countries; preaching engagements all over the world with confirmed schedules up to two years; and multi-faceted ministerial projects amounting to well over fifteen million dollars?'

They are anxious for answers, desirous to know the truth, keen to take the big step to new heights of success and prosperity in Christ. I simply tell them, 'The keys to success and prosperity are *grace, faith* and *hard work.*'

There is no real success without God's grace. There is no real success without faith in Him. And so there is no real success without corresponding hard work through grace and faith. Meditate deeply upon these words.

Now read this: 'Behold, the Lord your God has set the land before you: *go up and possess it* . . . . Fear not, neither be discouraged' (Deut 1.21). God earmarked a land for conquest by the children of Israel. God does not spoonfeed His children, and that is what many Christians ought to understand. God set the land before them. The life of success is one of going forward to possess our possessions. It has been said that God's will does not send a man to where His grace cannot sustain him. God's will and His grace go hand in hand.

It was God who set the land before them, so obviously His will was for the Israelites to claim it. As His will, so His grace! By His will and by His grace!

Remember this was a specific word they had to obey, not just listen to. *Go up! Possess it!* That sounds like a hard commandment. Yes, it was; God's 'go up' means just that. Many people have died without carrying out the vision or dream through delays. It took faith for the Israelites to go up and possess it, faith based on absolute trust and implicit belief in

God Who had commissioned them. They acted on the Word of the Lord, which is what I have done all these years. God has proved Himself faithful to the utmost.

Faith to go forward

Do you have faith to go forward and do what God has told you? What are you waiting for? Go up *now*! Faith clears all obstacles before it. The Israelites acquired the land, possessed the domain and God blessed them in all that they did through their hard work. They did not enter the land and sit down gazing at the sky. They worked hard to occupy the territory.

Do you still remember the master keys we mentioned—grace, faith and hard work?

We all love interesting stories and I wish to share one with you, one that will lead to renewed zeal to have faith in God at all times. When the Church of God Mission International Incorporated moved from its mother church (Iyaro) to the Miracle Centre in 1975, many spectacular events took place. Primarily this was a giant step of faith for a new, growing ministry. There were many who shook their heads in awe and exclaimed, 'Your faith is bigger than you!' I did not object to this accolade; I defied many threats in the initial stages and rather than deter me these goaded me on to higher grounds.

Some time in 1975 the government announced high-level steps to demolish the Miracle Centre. The reason given was that the church was too close to Benin Airport. A decree was accordingly passed to effect the demolition. I considered this move but a big joke. My mind recollected the time, money, effort and energy the church had expended. 'Shall we vacate the site?' some half-hearted Christians asked me. I told the church plainly, 'We shall see what manner of caterpillar would come here and destroy the house of God.'

Together in fellowship the church prayed and work continued steadily. (Read the example in Nehemiah 4.17.) With all my heart I believed God had established Miracle Centre and so no man could pull it down. The conclusion of the whole matter was that decree No. 46 of April 6, 1976, fizzled out and no caterpillar has yet come!

Resistance

Then came the resistance of the natives occupying portions of land close to the Miracle Centre. The land occupied by these natives had served as a fetish site for Benin monarchs from time immemorial. They therefore considered the land and site sacred. They were determined to die in defence of this portion of land. But I needed it for the work of the Lord because 'the earth is the Lord's and the fulness thereof; the world and they that dwell therein' (Ps 24.1).

One chilly morning I drove to the compound of the eldest occupant of this tract of land. 'Please sir, I want to buy this land you are occupying, to use as part of Miracle Centre. I will offer you a handsome payment,' I said, pointing across the piece of land.

'I will consider it with my colleagues,' he said with a note of triumph in his voice.

A week or so later I repeated the call. 'We would have sold it,' he lamented, 'but you know our groves and shrines are all here.'

I brightened up with a victorious smile and replied, 'If that is the only reason, leave that to me.' To myself I hummed, 'Is it demons that will stop me from accomplishing the purpose of God in the earth? —God forbid.'

In a matter of days I paid for the land and called in a bulldozer under my personal supervision to clear the site, including the groves and shrines. 'You cannot destroy this shrine,' some unbelieving natives yelled out. 'Come and see,' I replied calmly. Within hours the shrine lay in ruins, a shattered vestige of a helpless superstition. The students of the All Nations for Christ Bible Institute, Benin City, laboured a whole day clearing the debris of broken pots and graven images. We set the images of the grove on fire.

During the week that followed this demonstration of faith I prayed many nights for God's direction about what to do on the new site. At midnight God woke me up and said, 'My son Benson, go up and build a house of prayer on the exact spot where you removed the grove.' When I hear the voice of God, I don't ask questions; without ado I proceed on the mission in *grace, faith and hard work*. God's unfailing grace provided every dollar and naira for this challenging project. My faith in Him kept me going day and night in hope, believing we would see the fulfilment of the divine commission. With toil, determination and hard work a beautiful edifice stands today at the Miracle Centre with the bold inscription, 'The House of Prayer.'

On New Year's Day, 1986, thousands of members gathered to dedicate this building. It stands at the edge of a very busy road and all eyes see it and give glory to God for His mighty works in our midst.

Every facility for comfort was provided in the House of Prayer. A special telephone system was installed to meet the growing need of the people of God all over the world. The various ministries of Church of God Mission Int. Inc. (Miracle Centre) were provided with separate furnished offices. Among them were the Elders, Pastors, Soldiers of Christ, Ushers, Christian Women Fellowship International (CWFI) and prayer cell rooms, in addition to a spacious conference room for ministries. This was yet another living testimony of what faith in God can do, a fascinating story which gives credence to the walk of faith in our ministry, which yields manifold fruits of success.

14

UNDERSTANDING SUCCESS AND PROSPERITY

No good thing will He withhold from them that walk uprightly.

Psalm 84.11

Riches in a limited sense may be associated only with money and the possession of material things, but success means more than this. By the grace of God I can humbly speak *on* riches and *of* success.

During my ministry I have witnessed preachers and Christians alike expressing acid dislike of anything which smacks of prosperity. In several countries the storm is still raging in Pentecostal circles over teaching on prosperity. Many salvoes have been fired over the issue of Christianity and prosperity, to the point of labelling some men of God as 'prosperity preachers.' That in itself is a misnomer. A man who teaches and preaches prosperity is bringing to light a vital part of the Word of God which has been watered down through ignorance and lack of proper understanding. I have pinpointed two reasons why men of God do not teach and preach on prosperity; they are *ignorance* and *lack of under-*

standing of God's Word on this crucial issue.

We can examine a few salient verses from the Bible, not in isolation or out of context but within the whole framework of the revealed Word of God, significantly in the New Testament.

Jesus Christ, the Chief Shepherd (1 Pet 5.4) and Head of the church (Eph 1.22), did not mince words on an issue as important as the church and prosperity, for His disciples and followers have not completed their sojourn on this earth. I admit Christ warned against trusting in riches. That is to say, you can have money but don't let your money have you. The Lord stated unequivocably that the inordinate pursuit of riches is a highway to soul disaster. The stringent warning of Jesus Christ led the disciples to raise the obvious question, 'Who then can be saved?' (Mt 19.25).

But was Jesus putting poverty on a pedestal and urging His followers to spurn all forms of temporal possessions? The Lord Jesus Christ did not mean or teach that. In apparent alarm, Peter said to Jesus, 'Lo, we have left all and have followed thee' (Mk 10.28). The Lord immediately made a statement you must carefully examine. He said, 'Verily I say unto you, There is no man that hath left house or brethren or sisters or lands *for my sake and the Gospel's, but he shall receive a hundredfold now in this time, houses* and *brethren* and sisters, and mothers and children, and *lands,* with persecutions; and in the world to come eternal life. But many that are first shall be last; and the last first' (Mk 10.29–31). Any man or woman who reads these verses without prejudice will establish in plain language that the Lord promised temporal wealth.

God honours His Word

There is no confusion, my friend. Jesus says to you, 'No man that hath left house . . . or lands *for my sake* and the Gospel's, but he shall receive an hundredfold now in this time.' God honours His Word in any nation on the earth, from the United States of America to Africa and Asia. When you become born again, eternal life is assured, but in the labour of the Gospel on earth God promises temporal blessings.

God told me many years ago, 'I will make you an example to all the world in your generation, giving blessings and success both in the ministry and your family.' I have enough to know God is true.

Many people don't care to read the Bible to find out what exactly God's Word declares on a given issue; they go about as carriers of second-hand information. The Word of God encourages us: 'Be not conformed to this world, but be ye transformed by the renewing of your minds . . . and perfect will of God' (Rom 12.2). Many people, among them ungrounded Christians, are still conformed to this world. They read the Word of God but it is not allowed to renew their mind.

Religion in many countries and societies has done more harm than good. It has taught poor simple folks doctrines directly at variance with the Scriptures. Religion has been opposed to the healing ministry which the Bible highlights. It was so in the days of Jesus and the story has not changed today. The religious leaders confronted Jesus because He healed the man with the withered hand on a Sabbath day (see Mark 3). They considered the institution of the Sabbath day far more important than the sufferings of the sick man. The hypocrisy of religion cries to heaven!

In John 11 we see how the religious 'big shots' came to mourn the death of Lazarus; they were sad, or so it appeared. They even said, in John 11.37, 'Could not this man, which opened the eyes of the blind, have caused that even this man (Lazarus) should not have died?' Yet those religious men who a few hours before had been mourning and wailing, planned to kill Lazarus when Jesus raised him from the dead (Jn 12.10). Just imagine such wickedness. They wanted Lazarus in the grave. The spirit of religion still puts men into bondage. The Gospel sets men free (Gal 5.1).

In the area of success and prosperity, religion has provided millions with an erroneous conception built on superstition, man-made doctrines, ignorance, illiteracy and lack of scriptural revelation of God's Word. Therefore to enable you to come to a total grasp of the principles of success and prosperity, get rid of superstition, man-made doctrines, ignorance and illiteracy and have your eyes anointed to read and understand the precious Word, which is able to make you wise.

Religion in all cases associates poverty with piety; suffering with holiness; and burdens with humility. That is pure religious stuff and not the full Gospel message as presented by Jesus Christ (Jn 10.10). My dear friend, don't ask for prosperity if you will not use it for God. This has been my maxim whenever I think of prosperity in Christ.

A close examination of the Scriptures in Mark 10.29–31 will indicate that the great promise of the hundredfold blessing that Christ has given in His

Word was for those who in their heart have 'left all' and followed Him. In the outworking of God's purpose, the supreme demand is total consecration.

It is sad to consider that many people block the free flow of God's blessing and prosperity by their wrong attitude towards it. If you realise that temporal blessings are not intended for personal gratification, you will go a long way. Every believer is a steward!

Stewardship of money

By the grace of God, I have experienced nearly three decades of successful ministry. Among the great lessons I have been taught by God is that of stewardship and giving. Whenever we talk about tithes and offerings, some Christians develop running stomachs and goose pimples. It is a sad spectacle. From the beginning of my ministry I have honoured God with my tithes and offerings, up to 90 per cent of our family earnings. Today more than ever before God needs men and women of means and substance, dedicated people who can give to the cause of the Gospel at all times. Such men and women are few, but they are prosperous and exceedingly successful, regardless of where they are.

There is one important factor we must always bear in mind—times have changed. Man may not have changed, but conditions have changed. Technological innovations bounce on to mankind with incredible speed. In every area of life knowledge has widened. Transport by land, sea and air has accelerated alarmingly. Mass communication equipment of all kinds is being devised. And without doubt the most noticeable phenomenon in our time is the explosive increase in population everywhere, particularly in the so-called Third World.

How can we preach the Gospel of Jesus Christ in the fastest time at our disposal? We live in time and space, and every minute counts for life or death to a soul somewhere.

If you have compassion in your heart, the figures I present here which I read recently in a magazine should paint a gruesome picture of the need of the hour. The world population is estimated at around 4.7 billion. About one billion name Jesus as Lord, of whom 200 million are committed and 800 million are nominal. Altogether those who have heard of Jesus make up another one billion. Those who have never heard the Gospel at all are in the region of 2.7 billion. The statistics show that there are 7,000 missionaries labouring among these people—a ratio of 1:450,000! There are 7,000 living languages in the world, of which 5,199 still have no Bible. At the present rate of population growth and growth through evangelism, by the year 2,000 our world will have seven billion people with nearly 5.2 billion unevangelised.

My friend, it is not for fun that I present these facts to you. Let your spirit be stirred up to see the task before us today. It is a task that must be performed. This onerous task calls for money and large resources. The people of God must do the work of God, using their time, money and resources. If there were many born-again, Spirit-filled Christian millionaires, what an opportunity it would offer for the total Gospel effort! Unbelievers misunderstand and oppose the Gospel. Sinners, whether rich or poor, are not willing to support the Gospel effort.

In June 1986 the Idahosa World Outreach held a historic Gospel crusade in Kano, the Islamic hotspot of Nigeria. As has become my custom, we chartered a special 10-seater executive jet from Okada Airlines (a private airline in Benin City, Nigeria). We made the journey from Benin City to Kano, in the northern part of Nigeria, in a little over an hour. The same plane brought us back for a Sunday morning service at the end of the crusade. It was a smooth trip without drudgery; but it would have taken not less than 12 hours by road. The Bible says, 'Redeem the time!' The Gospel must be preached now!

Using all the resources

At the international airport in Kano I drew my wife's attention to some Boeing jets on the tarmac: 'Honey, all these planes are owned by a Moslem, an unbeliever. What an advantage it would be to the Gospel effort to go round the world in our own plane proclaiming Jesus as Lord and Saviour.' She simply smiled and said, 'God is able.' Unbelievers and Moslems can own and operate airlines to carry them to Mecca, but when a Christian is prospered by God to own a plane, some men see it as carnal or sinful. Let us arise to the needs of the times. Let us use all the available means and resources that God has graciously provided to get the Gospel message over to a perishing world. Soon it will be too late.

All that I have been trying to establish is that God trusts men with temporal wealth and prosperity primarily for His work here on earth. If that vision is lost to the possessor, the result is tragic, with eternal consequences.

Year after year I have experienced abundant harvests far beyond my expectation. I have persuaded my family to sow in the harvest field of God. The normal church tithes and offerings have by all indications not been able to carry out some of the magnificent building projects in my ministry. A Bible school complex with nearly 500 students. A well-equipped television studio. Facilities for missionary residence. The 30,000-seater auditorium which observers believe would rank as the biggest stadium church on the continent of Africa. Many more projects are in the offing, including the vision of a Christian faith university for which land has already been acquired. Where do all the finances come from for these extensive projects? I exercise faith in my giving, over and above what the Scripture recommends. I see all money that comes to my evangelistic ministry as foremost a presentation to Christ who according to Hebrews 7.8 receives it from my hand. God rewards faithfulness, from the least to the greatest.

Beloved, do not postpone your giving to some future date. Now is the accepted time. Now! Now! A hundredfold interest awaits us as we act in faith. 'No good thing will He withhold from them that walk uprightly' (Ps 84.11).

What I have presented to you are grains of principles for understanding the Scriptural way to success and prosperity. The secret of faith is to plant the seed of belief.

15

FAITH WAY TO SUCCESS—ONE DAY AT A TIME

Pray without ceasing.
1 Thessalonians 5.17

We have spoken of success and prosperity within the confines of the revealed Word of God. I have good reason to know that the success God gives to a man in a large measure transcends money and material wealth; it is a way of life which demonstrates His glory and greatness. Our daily lives should reflect it in the eyes of a pessimistic world which is basking in bleakness and schemes.

This chapter is dedicated to all children of God who aspire to greatness, success and prosperity in the things of God. Let us call it the faith way to success. I want to describe to you, as best I can, the walk of faith I follow day by day.

The heroes and heroines of Hebrews 11 worshipped by faith, as Abel. They walked by faith, as Enoch. They laboured by faith, as Noah. Above all, they lived by faith, as Abraham. They governed by faith, as Moses. They followed the way of God by faith, as Israel. They fought by faith, as Joshua; conquered by faith, as Gideon; subdued kingdoms by faith, as David. They closed the mouths of lions by faith, as Daniel. Singing praises to God, they suffered by faith, as Paul. With holy devotion to the calling of God, these great men and women died by faith, as Stephen.

Through faith in Christ and by His grace I daily need to exhibit patience in suffering, strength in weakness and courage in the face of overwhelming odds, and to claim victory even when all hope seems lost. The secret is simple; I am more than a conqueror through Christ. The unyielding faith of the saints of past days offers me abounding inspiration, but I never forget to look to Jesus every day as the supreme example of faith.

In the corridors of power all over the world it is not uncommon to hear the familiar remark, 'Uneasy lies the head that wears the crown.' That is descriptive of the suspense, pressure and strain associated with authority, rulership and success. In my school days I thought of that phrase only in connection with unbelieving rulers, monarchs and leaders, but with nearly three decades of international and diverse exposure to the Lord's work, I have had deeper insight from both the Word of God and great men of God living today who are at the helm of ministerial responsibility.

Maybe we all agree that if a man or woman finds favour in the sight of God and is raised to a position of prominence and responsibility in His vineyard, His goodness, mercy and providence will also be part of the package. That is to say, God's hand of overflowing grace and sustenance will be readily available in the burden of a gigantic ministerial task.

Privilege and responsibility

But it is sobering to realise that in and out of the Bible, the shoulders of the servant of God still burn from the excruciating loads which accompany the privilege of being an elect of the Most High God. Privilege is followed by responsibility!

A vital key to success is that achievers risk their lives. Let us recall the memorable words of the author of the Reformation. He said with great wisdom, 'Too much folly is displeasing to men, but too much discretion is displeasing to God. The Gospel cannot be defended without tumult and with scandal.' These words should give you food for thought. Too much playing safe has destroyed the aspirations of men and women headed for success.

Success today by God's grace has become a byword in the international multi-faceted ministry I handle as Archbishop of Church of God Mission Int. Inc. and President of the Idahosa World Outreach Inc. I must not remove my eyes from Christ Who called me. The enormity of the job is shattering, but *grace, faith and hard work,* one day at a time, bring in eternal fruits.

Whenever I lecture in church growth conferences I find people who say something like, 'But Archbishop, you know that Church of God Mission Int. Inc. has come a long way.' Yes, no disputing this fact. We have learned to believe God more now than before. And so we can do more now than before. Please increase your faith in God.

Sometimes when I come across people who are amazed at the progress we have made, I testify to them: 'Friend, we are just beginning.' And I believe this should be your daily maxim. Regardless of the stage and height you have reached, still press forward.

When the Apostle Paul wrote Philippians 3.12–14, he had seen considerable success. But it was not enough for him. He wrote to the church he dearly loved: 'If by any means I might attain . . . Not as though *I had already attained,* either were already perfect, but I follow after, if that I may apprehend . . . Brethren, I count not myself to have apprehended . . . forgetting those things which are behind, and reaching forth unto those which are before, I press toward the mark for the prize of the high calling of God in Christ Jesus.' Paul was, in other words, saying, 'Today's maximum must be tomorrow's minimum.'

What do I have to contend with every day? Some 3,000 branches all over the world; Bible college; evangelism and missions; international crusades and church planting; correspondence; publications; television ministry; radio ministry; Word of Faith college; Miracle Faith Auditorium; missionaries' guest house project; and more. The very thought of it is humbling. Thousands of letters pour into Miracle Centre daily from all over the world. Many need my personal attention. His grace for success is sufficient.

Extensive travelling all through the year is no new feature, visiting some 80 countries. On the home front, how do I cope with a normal day at Miracle Centre, a hive of activity and a tourist attraction for people of all faiths?

In tune with God

From my bed, on my knees, across the balcony,

along the busy Lagos streets, far up in the air, I am in tune with God in the Spirit. That is walking in the Spirit!

It is 3.00 am, and I prepare myself for the day ahead. It is time to seek the face of the Lord. It is time to talk to my Sustainer and Master, time to seek needed answers to many issues. My heart stretches with compassion and a burden for souls whenever I wait upon God—it is the heart-throb of the Lord. Prayer and waiting upon the Lord in the midnight hour is the result of consistent self-discipline.

They that seek the Lord early shall find Him. With quivering lips and groaning spirit, in the dark hours you must knock on the door of God's throne room for the needs of people far and near. You must stand in the gap and make the hedge for the body of Christ, for marriages, ministries, aspirations of nations and the bold propagation of the Gospel of Christ.

You cannot hold back the dawn. The cocks begin to crow, the rays of light fight their way through the curtain announcing the arrival of a new day. The faithful clock atop my bedroom table gently sounds five times. My day starts at midnight, but five o'clock is the time to step out and possess the land.

I make my way to the dressing-room, shape up my body and tune up for the Lord's business. It is time to take the two-kilometre journey to Miracle Centre from my home, the Lord's 'Faith Mission.' Well over four years ago the Lord laid a burden on my heart which resulted in the morning devotional service, which today draws hundreds every morning.

Denunciation of witches

News reached me some time in December 1982 about a proposed international witches' conference in Benin City. I considered this move an affront to the ministry of Jesus Christ. We embarked on a crusade to oppose and abort this heinous meeting. Large-scale prayer sessions were started by thousands of believers in Nigeria. I took the fight a step further. I went on the national television network, denounced the faceless warlocks and called for an open media interview with them. On television I made a historic pronouncement: 'God placed me here for a purpose at such a time as this; I shall not fail in my duty to God. I make it known to the whole world that the international witches' conference in Benin City is dead and buried forever in the name of Jesus Christ, Whom I serve and Whose I am.'

The world sat in suspense, and nothing more was heard of the meeting. This event bore fruit in the daily morning devotional services at Miracle Centre, and the fire is still burning. The sound of singing and clapping from joyous God-hungry hearts is evident everywhere in Miracle Centre. My car pulls to a stop, I walk into the church and kneel down solemnly before the Lord at the altar. Hundreds more are on their knees everywhere in the sanctuary. Choruses and singing soon take over in increased tempo. As usual, I settle on the elevated part of the altar, facing the congregation.

It is 5.30 am. An associate minister, elder or deacon is appointed to present a brief exhortation. All is set. After a brief summary of the exhortation, prayer is offered and the curtain is lowered. We go into the world with one key verse, 'This is the day which the Lord hath made; we will rejoice and be glad in it' (Ps 118.24). I have always exhorted in the morning services, 'Friends, if you can defeat the devil by five o'clock you will be in charge the rest of the day.'

Parents from long distances begin to drive back with their children. The Bible school students who attend the morning service without option proceed to their daily assignments. A new day of promise has begun.

Many hundreds crowd around me for a handshake, warm greetings or discussion of some point. 'Hello Osagie, how is your father?' I ask someone close by. 'My beloved deacon, how is your wife and children?' I share love, smiles and encouragement with all the people. Whatsoever a man soweth that shall he also reap. Sow love and reap love. Sow joy and reap joy. Sow encouragement and reap encouragement. Whatsoever you sow, it will come to you a hundredfold according to the Word of God.

By the grace of God I recognise the faces and names of thousands of people. There is something in calling a friend by his name. Walking through the morning crowd, I bless them with blessings of God.

It is 6.45 am. A day of activity has unfolded. It is time to share the Word of God on the family front. The children gather; they make rich and beautiful contributions. I give them an opportunity to preach to myself and Margaret. Holy hands are joined in unity of faith and prayers are offered for God's mercy, grace and leading, every minute of the day. This is a family that knows how to wait on God. Gradually and reverently, singing and choruses ring out from every lip. It is a harmonious melody of voices—a family knit in affection and inseparable love for Christ our Lord.

It is 9.00 am. Visitors are already pouring into our home. The Miracle Centre international office operates a 24-hour round-the-clock schedule of personal and telephone counselling. The international office is spick and span; every blade of grass shines with the glory of God as the morning rays light up the enchanting scenery. The international office houses the administrative headquarters of the Church of God Mission Int. Inc., Oral Roberts Evangelistic Association (OREA), Idahosa World Outreach Inc. (IWO Nigeria), and others.

The corridors of the main reception hall are as usual crowded with people this morning, from all over the country. They have travelled long distances from Lagos (300km), Calabar (500km), or Sokoto (1,500km), or as close as Benin City. Some have spent days in transit, but their faith is unwavering.

It is 9.30 am. Picking up the telephone I get through to my hospitality secretary, Rev Hannah Arthur. 'Hello, this is the Archbishop speaking. I shall be in the office in 15 minutes time. Thank you and God bless you.' The atmosphere is charged with expectation.

It is 10.00 am—a morning of hope and blessings in the Lord. I drive into the parking booth. An intense survey brings me a picture of every activity. I wave to a few visitors coming and going, shaking many hands along the way.

Success brings honour and we give God the glory. The light is on, the air-conditioner hums away dutifully. My first job in the office is to pray for guidance and wisdom from the Lord in every decision and ministration. Prayer must be your way of life, then success will overtake you.

Counsel and prayer
A mountainous heap of international and local mail awaits me. Hundreds of typed letters await my signature. Silently I pray over them and append my signature—a miracle is on the way to someone far or near. The two hotline telephones on my table ring intermittently, bringing glad tidings from all over the world—Australia, the United States, Lagos, or even nearby Benin City. Meanwhile the ordained ministers on duty have a busy time counselling visitors and praying for the needs of hundreds of people who call at the Miracle Centre. High government officials, top-flight businessmen, prominent social figures and other Christian leaders call daily by appointment.

It is 12.00 noon. Whenever possible I find time to lecture students of the All Nations for Christ Bible Institute in Benin City. News reaches the Bible school students of my readiness to share the Word of God with them. They hurry up and down to get equipment ready. Interestingly, many of the visitors rush to join the students.

It is 1.00 pm and time to go home for lunch. 'Hello honey, this is Margaret; lunch is ready, thank you,' my wife occasionally calls from home. Thank God for good wives; they are worth more than rubies. In the spirit of a good wife and mother, Reverend Dr Mrs Margaret Idahosa, who also has offices at Miracle Centre, has gone ahead to get meals ready for us. There is the usual crowd of visitors at the Lord's Faith Mansion, with cars parked in many places on the vast premises. We share the lunch with all the visitors. My personal policy is for visitors to eat before they leave our home, and I sometimes tell them, 'Blessed be the Lord who has set a table before me in the presence of my friends.'

It is a profound blessing to have courteous, God-fearing children (Prov 22.6). Our children are brought up to put comfort, love, a smile, respect and cheer into the heart of everyone who calls at our home. They love people!

It is 4.00 pm and evening service is two hours away. Time for a break, a moment of rest and meditation. Up into bed, fellowshipping with the Lord in silent prayers, reading the Word of God or a new Christian book or novel.

It is 6.00 pm. The whole family is set for evening service. Miracle Centre is a place where God is always doing something new with His people. What is it? Just stop and listen. It is the coordinated sound of trumpets, drums, flutes and the melodic combination of harmonious voices introducing to your ears the inimitable Christian Redeemed Voices Choir. The crescendo of voices from the prayer room tells you of the ever-ready prayer band led by Elder John Idahosa, my senior brother.

Students of the All Nations for Christ Bible Institute and the rest of the congregation clap and sing in the main chapel in preparation for the service. Prayer here, prayer there, prayer everywhere, a key secret of the glittering success at Miracle Centre. The worship gathers momentum; voices are lifted up in total surrender to God.

It is 7.00 pm. With Margaret, I walk into a church ready for God's Word in the now. As I am introduced to preach, I submit to the power of the Holy Spirit: 'Lord, your mighty anointing is ever available to break every yoke and bless your people. Through me do your work. Glory is yours.' The message goes forth in the power of His might, needs are met by His grace and lives are blessed with His Word.

It is 8.00 pm. The sermon is over and the crowd flows out into the moonlight. I spend some time saying 'goodnights' and 'how are yous.' A shepherd has need of patience and endurance if he is to succeed, by God's grace. Night is drawing nigh. The crowd keeps coming. Time to go home.

It is 9.00 pm. Supper time for all the family and visitors. Callers keep ringing in. The clock sounds at 10.00 pm and it's time for family prayer preparatory to sleep. God's winning team must learn to fight on its knees.

'Goodnight Daddy, goodnight Mummy.' The children make their way to bed. I spend some time discussing, counselling and praying with late-night visitors. You cannot hold the dawn and also the dusk. Sleep prepares the body with freshness for a new day ahead. God gives His beloved a sound sleep.

I have tried to show you how God gives me grace

to live one day at a time at home. Major changes may occur to alter the arrangements for any day, but our heart's desire is to live each day for Christ and His Kingdom, in selfless surrender to His will and calling.

Beloved, God is faithful, who will not suffer you to fail. Live for Him one day at a time; He will prosper the labour of your hands.

Jesus Christ and you!

A sinner's prayer to accept Jesus as Lord and Saviour

Our God and Father in heaven: I come before your throne in Jesus' name. Your Word says that 'All have sinned and come short of the glory of God' (Romans 3.23), and that 'The wages of sin is death' (Romans 6.23). But you also say in your Word that, 'Whosoever shall call upon the Name of the Lord shall be saved' (Romans 10.13). I am calling on you to save me now!

You have said, 'If thou shalt confess with thy mouth the Lord Jesus, and shalt believe in thine heart that God hath raised Him from the dead, thou shalt be saved. For with the heart man believeth unto righteousness; and with the mouth confession is made unto salvation' (Romans 10.9–10).

I believe in my heart that Jesus Christ is the Son of God who died for my sins, and that He was raised for my justification. I confess Him now as my Saviour and Lord.

Hallelujah! I have now become the righteousness of God in Christ (2 Corinthians 5.21)! Praise the Lord, I am saved!

Signed ....

Name and address ....

....

....

Date ....